SCENES FOR TWO

Book I
Duologues for Young Players

Edited by

MARY GREENSLADE
and
ANNE HARVEY

Samuel French — London
New York — Sydney — Toronto — Hollywood

CONTENTS

CONTENTS

CONTENTS

CONTENTS

AUTHORS' INDEX

ACKNOWLEDGEMENTS

FOR permission to reprint copyright material in this anthology the compilers and publishers are grateful to the following authors, authors' representatives, and publishers:

Enid Bagnold: the Author

Wilbur Braun: the Author and Samuel French Inc.

Alice Chadwicke: the Author and Samuel French Inc.

Elizabeth Fuller Chapman: the Author and Samuel French Inc.

Jerome Chodorov and Joseph Fields: Jerome Chodorov and the Estate of Joseph Fields

John Galsworthy: (from *Ten Famous Plays*) Gerald Duckworth and Co Ltd

Rumer Godden: the Author, Macmillan and Co Ltd and Nan Macdonald

Nicholas Stuart Gray: the Author and Oxford University Press

Willis Hall: the Author and Blackie and Son Ltd

Frances Hodgson Burnett: the executors of the Frances Hodgson Burnett estate and (from *A Little Princess*) Frederick Warne and Co Ltd and (from *The Secret Garden*) William Heinemann Ltd

Eric Jones-Evans: the Author and G. F. Wilson and Co Ltd

Carson McCullers: the Author and Ashley Famous Agency Inc.

Maurice Maeterlinck: the Translator and Methuen and Co Ltd

Suria Magito and Rudolph Weil: the Authors and Heinemann Educational Books Ltd

Lillian and Robert Masters: the Authors and Samuel French Inc.

A. A. Milne: the executors of the A. A. Milne estate

Eugene O'Neill: the executors of the Eugene O'Neill estate and Jonathan Cape Ltd

Roland Pertwee: the Author and English Theatre Guild Ltd

Michael Redgrave: the Author

Johanna Spyri: Beryl M. Jones and Sir Isaac Pitman and Sons Ltd

Aimee Stuart: the Author

Joan Temple: the Author and Sampson Low, Marston and Co Ltd

J. C. Trewin: the Author and Elek Books

Alison Uttley: the Author and Faber and Faber Ltd

Barbara Watts: the Author and Peter Davis Ltd

Brian Way and Warren Jenkins: the Authors and Dennis Dobson Publishers

INTRODUCTION

THE persistent cry of "Can you suggest a new scene for us—please?" convinced us of the need for this book, and other teachers, who shared this problem of lack of fresh acting material, greeted the idea with enthusiasm.

This book, the first of two volumes, contains a selection of scenes suitable for girls and boys up to fifteen years of age.

Our own young students have read, experimented with and rejected or acclaimed all our suggestions. We have valued their criticism. Fantasy, adaptations from literature, period and modern drama are all included. Our choice is not restricted to juvenile writing, for much adult drama offers parts for young people, and the more mature themes are rewarding, particularly for the older age group. We have tried to select scenes that have dramatic impact and well-developed character relationships; scenes to stretch the imagination. Where necessary a short introduction explains the context, but this is no real substitute for studying the whole play.

Private Speech and Drama teachers will use the extracts for performance in festivals and examinations, and Youth Clubs should find them invaluable. We ourselves have used them with large oral English and Drama classes in schools, in the following ways:

1. The class is divided into groups of four. Two girls act each scene and two work as producer and stage manager.
2. The scenes are read or performed, and the class then discusses them. Discussion can cover dramatic situation and writing, character, costume, production and staging.
3. The scenes may be used as a starting point for written and oral improvisation.

We hope that whichever way the book is used it will provide enjoyment as well as instruction.

May we here offer our thanks to Mr Noel Woolf for his help and patience, and to our drama pupils at Notting Hill and Ealing High School for Girls, GPDST and The Holy Cross Convent School, New Malden, for being our guinea-pigs.

THE ADVENTURES OF TOM SAWYER

By WILBUR BRAUN
From the novel by MARK TWAIN

Mrs Douglas, a short, stout, asthmatic woman in her late forties, visits Aunt Polly, who is a tall and angular woman of fifty, with whom Tom lives.

SCENE—*Aunt Polly's home in St. Petersburg, Missouri.*

TIME—*1880 or thereabouts.*

AUNT POLLY (*as she enters* L, *loudly*) Tom—Oh, Tom Sawyer! What's gone with that boy, I wonder? Oh, you, T-o-m-m! (*She sniffs the air unpleasantly as though she had detected a foul odour, crosses to* C *and stands continuing to sniff*) My, there's somethin' mighty unpleasant smellin' in this house. (*Raising her voice again and turning to search the room*) Tom! Lan's, I never did see the beat of that boy.

(AUNT POLLY *lowers her spectacles to her eyes, crosses up to the table* RC, *lifts the covering and peers underneath the table. A loud knocking is heard on the* C *door. She drops the table covering, raises her spectacles so that they rest on her forehead, crosses up* C *and opens the door*)

MRS DOUGLAS (*as she stands in the doorway, whiningly*) I just thought I'd drop in an' set fer awhile, Polly. I've been doin' some shoppin' an' I give out so easy.

AUNT POLLY (*taking* R *a few steps*) Come right in an' set, Widder Douglas. You need a dose of my pain-killer. That'll fix you up all right. (*She crosses* R *to whatnot*)

MRS DOUGLAS (*entering and closing the door; shudderingly*) None o' that pain-killer for me, Polly. The last time you give me some it nigh knocked the life outa me. (*She crosses to sofa* LC *and sits*)

AUNT POLLY (*coming down* R *of the table and consulting one of her almanacs*) Here's the very thing for you. Cook's Sulphur Syrup—bound to rid you o' that tired feelin'. You'd oughta send for a bottle right away. (*She crosses to* C *and leafs through the almanac*) Maybe I got somethin' in the kitchen that'll help you to feel better. (*She starts for the door* L)

MRS DOUGLAS (*half rising; fearfully*) Hold on, Polly. You needn't go to no trouble for me. I ain't takin' no more medicines in this house.

AUNT POLLY (*pausing down* L *and facing her*) And why not, pray?

MRS DOUGLAS (*whiningly*) 'Tain't safe, that's why. (*She sinks back*

I

on to the sofa) That Tom Sawyer might 'a' put poison in them bottles without you knowin' it.

AUNT POLLY (*crossing to* C; *haughtily*) Tom wouldn't do no such thing.

MRS DOUGLAS (*knowingly*) Oh, wouldn't he now?

AUNT POLLY (*vigorously*) I should say he wouldn't. (*She crosses to the chair* L *of the table and sits; stiffly*) Oh, I'll admit he's a bit mischievous and he does try my patience at times. But he's so lovable that I just can't stay mad at him nohow.

MRS DOUGLAS (*whiningly*) He's the very worst boy in this town. Him an' that Huckleberry Finn . . .

AUNT POLLY (*breaking in quickly*) Tom don't have nothin' to do with Huck since I forbade him to speak to him.

(MRS DOUGLAS *opens her mouth as though to speak but* AUNT POLLY *continues before she has a chance*)

You forget, Widder, that Tom Sawyer is my dead sister's boy and I'm the only mother he's ever known.

MRS DOUGLAS (*facing her*) Sid Sawyer is Tom's half-brother and he's had no easier time than Tom. But look at the diff'rence in them two boys. Sid is the model boy of the town.

AUNT POLLY (*pridefully*) And Tom is another model boy—or leastways he will be. (*Picking up the Bible from the table and holding it up for Mrs Douglas to see*) You see this Bible? My Tom got this yesterday for havin' twelve yeller tickets. And twelve yeller tickets means that he had more merit marks than any other boy in Sunday School.

MRS DOUGLAS (*whiningly*) I wouldn'ta believed it if you hadn't told me so, Polly. There musta been a mistake made some place.

AUNT POLLY (*angrily*) No mistake 'bout it. Judge Thatcher gave this Bible to my Tom and he made a right nice speech along with it. He expects Tom to be a big lawyer one o' these days.

MRS DOUGLAS (*pressing her lips together; dubiously*) I don't expect to live that long. Every time I see them boys, Huck Finn an' your Tom, together, I say to myself, say I, "Widder, you're lucky you never had no children to raise."

AUNT POLLY (*brusquely*) Maybe if you did have you wouldn't have so much time on your hands to think o' your diff'rent ailments.

MRS DOUGLAS (*indignantly*) Well, I like that! An' everybody in town knows that you support Ira Hamburg's Drug Store by buyin' patent medicines.

AUNT POLLY (*banging the Bible down on the table and rising*) 'Tain't so. I ain't bought a bottle of medicine from that man . . .

MRS DOUGLAS (*breaking in nervously*) But I tell you Ira Hamburg sez—er—that is—Ira Hamburg—er . . .

AUNT POLLY (*standing facing her with her hands on her hips; angrily*) Oh, *smother* Hamburg. You come here to rest, not to fight. I'll never buy another thing from that man again.

MRS DOUGLAS (*rising*) I just wanted to ask you if . . . (*She pauses abruptly and sniffs the air unpleasantly*) Goodness, gracious me, Polly. What smells so awful in here? I'm gettin' actually faint from it! (*She resumes her seat on the sofa*)

AUNT POLLY (*sniffing the air again*) Oh, so you notice it too, do you?

MRS DOUGLAS (*holding her nose and contorting her features*) Notice it? Why, it's simply turrible!

AUNT POLLY (*with a grimace*) 'Tain't half as bad in here as 'tis in there. (*She points to the door* R) I've searched through every room in the house and I can't find a thing that'd account for it.

MRS DOUGLAS (*whiningly*) I'll bet that Tom Sawyer'd know if you could only get the truth outa him.

AUNT POLLY (*crossing to the chair and resuming her seat*) Fiddlesticks! Tom ain't got nothin' to do with this. I tell you he's turned over a new leaf. He ain't even mischievous any more.

MRS DOUGLAS (*settling back on the sofa; derisively*) You mean he's coverin' up his mischief better'n he usedta. Now if you was to tell me 'bout Sid bein' a perfect gentleman . . .

AUNT POLLY (*breaking in quickly and picking up the Bible from the table*) I was never so proud over anythin' as I am about Tom's gettin' this Bible. If only my poor dear sister could be here to know what a fine boy her Tom is turnin' out to be.

MRS DOUGLAS (*whiningly*) Somethin' tells me that it's just as well she ain't. (*Rising*) Oh, my goodness, I just gotta get outa here. That odour is somethin' awful!

THE ADVENTURES OF TOM SAWYER

Tom is a mischievous boy in his middle teens, and Becky is his age, refined and charming.

SCENE—*The sitting-room of Aunt Polly's home in Missouri.*

BECKY (*enters* C *from* L *carrying a small brooch in her hand*) Oh, it's you, is it, Tom Sawyer? (*She greets him coldly*)

TOM (*gazing at her admiringly*) Come on in, Becky. I was just going to hunt you up over at your house.

BECKY (*taking a few steps down* C; *frigidly*) You can save yourself the trouble. Alfred Temple is waiting outside for me.

TOM (*coming to* L *of her, folding the paper and placing it in his trouser pocket*) Alfred Temple! Ha! You don't mean to say that you'd pay any attention to that baby, do you?

BECKY (*haughtily*) Alfred Temple has manners. And that's more than I can say for some people.

TOM (*wrathfully*) He won't have anything left by the time I get through with him. I'll lam him all over the place if he don't stay away from you.

BECKY (*drawing herself up to her full height*) Oh, yes, you will—I guess you'll think twice before you do anything like that.

TOM (*anxiously*) What have you got a mad on against me for, Beck? I ain't done nothing.

BECKY (*condescendingly*) When a gentleman has an engagement to call on a lady and fails to appear at the proper time the lady never speaks to the gentleman again. (*Takes over* R *a few steps and turns her back on him*)

TOM (*following her*) Aw, shucks, Becky, I wanted to come to see you last night, honest I did, but I just couldn't get away.

BECKY (*without turning*) If you want me to forgive you you'll have to think of a better reason than that, Tom Sawyer.

TOM (*frowningly*) Well, give me time, can't you?

BECKY (*turning on him angrily*) I'm not interested in anything you say or do. I didn't come over here to see you.

TOM (*disappointedly*) You didn't?

BECKY (*haughtily*) I should say not. Your Aunt Polly left this brooch at our house last night and my mamma insisted that I bring it over. (*She hands him the brooch*) See that she gets it, please. (*She starts for the door* C)

TOM (*rushing up and standing in front of the doorway, blocking her exit; pleadingly*) Listen, Becky. Please forgive me. I ain't never thought so much about any girl before.

4

BECKY (*softening a little*) I don't believe a word of it, Tom Sawyer.

TOM (*ardently*) It's true, honest it is. Why, I'd even wear a necktie for you. (*Pleadingly*) If you'll only forgive me I'll give you my tooth that Aunt Polly pulled out, and I wouldn't part with that to no one else but you. (*He reaches into his trouser pocket as though to bring his tooth out*)

BECKY (*haughtily*) I don't want your old tooth, Tom Sawyer. Let me out of here.

TOM (*without moving*) I guess you'll be sorry you acted this way when I join the circus and get to be a real clown.

BECKY (*greatly awed*) What?

TOM (*seizing his advantage*) You won't be sorry much, will you? Oh, no!

BECKY (*terribly impressed*) We-el, maybe I was a little hasty but . . .

TOM (*breaking in quickly*) Will you promise not to try to go out this door if I show you something?

BECKY (*eagerly*) What is it?

TOM (*firmly*) You've got to promise not to try to leave first.

BECKY (*agog with curiosity*) All right, I promise. Show it to me. (*She hops from one foot to the other excitedly*)

TOM (*realizing that the battle is almost won*) And will you promise that you'll never speak to Alfred Temple again?

BECKY (*hesitatingly*) We-el—I—er . . .

TOM (*breaking in quickly*) If you don't promise right here and now I won't show it to you—not ever.

BECKY (*her curiosity overcoming her*) All right. I promise. Now what is it?

TOM (*persistently*) You've got to promise like you really mean it.

BECKY (*solemnly*) Deed and deed and double deed, I promise.

TOM (*jubilantly*) Then look at this! (*He rushes over R to the whatnot and brings forth a bright, shiny brass knob, then crosses to R of her, holding it up pridefully*) Ain't it a beauty?

BECKY (*disappointedly*) Is that all you've got to show me?

TOM (*protestingly*) All? Why, there ain't another boy in town that has a brass and iron knob like this, Becky. Honest there ain't. I could get four peanut bars and a bag of popcorn thrown in for this doorknob.

BECKY (*irately*) And I thought you had something real wonderful to show me. Tom Sawyer, I take back my promise.

TOM (*bewilderedly*) But, Becky, I . . .

BECKY (*breaking in, tauntingly*) Alfred Temple has a real live pony and he's going to teach me how to ride.

TOM (*striving to conceal the hurt*) Aw, shucks, what's a pony? I guess I'll have more'n one pony when I get to be a robber. I'll have a whole slew of 'em.

BECKY (*wrathfully*) I don't care what you have. Give that brooch to your auntie and don't bother me ever again. A brass and iron knob indeed! (*She rushes out C to L*)

TOM (*rushing up to the doorway and calling off* L) Hey, Becky, come back. I got something else to show you. Come back here. (*There is a breathless pause. Then he turns slowly, lowers his head and crosses over to the whatnot, muttering to himself*) Let her go. See if I care. Girls are all alike. The minute you show 'em you care for 'em they walk out on you. (*He places the brass knob back in the whatnot, crosses to* C *and kicks the floor savagely*) I'm through with girls for ever!

ALL GOD'S CHILLUN GOT WINGS

By EUGENE O'NEILL

This is the prologue to an adult play dealing with the colour problem in New York in the 1920's. Jim, a Negro boy, and Ella, a white girl, eventually get married, but their story ends in tragedy.

SCENE—*A New York street.*

ELLA, *about eight years old, is crying.* JIM, *older, comes to her.*

JIM. Don't bawl no more. I done chased 'em.

ELLA. Thanks.

JIM. It was a cinch. I kin wipe up de street wid any one of dem. Feel dat muscle.

ELLA. My! (*Gingerly at first*)

JIM. You mustn't never be scared when I'm hanging around, Painty Face.

ELLA. Don't call me that, Jim, please.

JIM. I don't mean nothing. I didn't know you'd mind.

ELLA. I do . . . more'n anything.

JIM. You oughtn't to mind. Dey's jealous, dat's what.

ELLA. Jealous? Of what?

JIM. Of dat. (*He points to her face*) Red'n white. It's purty.

ELLA. I hate it.

JIM. It's purty. Yes, it's . . . purty. It's outa sight.

ELLA. I hate it. I wish I was black like you.

JIM. No, you don't. Dey'd call you Crow, den—or Chocolate . . . or Smoke.

ELLA. I wouldn't mind.

JIM. Dey'd call you nigger sometimes too.

ELLA. I wouldn't mind.

JIM. You wouldn't mind?

ELLA. No, I wouldn't mind.

(*Pause*)

JIM. You know what, Ella? Since I bin tuckin' yo' books to school and back, I bin drinkin' lots o' chalk 'n water three times a day. Dat Tom, de barber, he tole me dat makes me white if I drinks enough. (*Pleading*) Does I look whiter?

ELLA. Yes—maybe—a little bit . . .

JIM. Reckon dat Tom's a liar and de jokes on me! Dat chalk only makes me feel kinda sick inside.

ELLA. Why do you want to be white?

7

Jim. Because . . . just because I lak dat better.

Ella. I wouldn't. I like black. Let's you and me swap. I'd like to be black. Gee that'd be fun, if we only could!

Jim. Ye-s—maybe . . .

Ella. Then they'd call me Crow and you'd be Painty Face!

Jim. They wouldn't never dast call you nigger, you bet! I'd kill 'em!

(*Pause. She takes his hand*)

Ella. I like you.

Jim. I like you.

Ella. Do you want to be my feller?

Jim. Yes.

Ella. Then I'm your girl.

Jim. Yes. You kin bet none of de gang gwine call you Painty Face from dis out! I lam 'em good.

(*They stand hand in hand. It is growing dark*)

Ella. Golly, it's late. I'll get a lickin'.

Jim. Me, too.

Ella. I won't mind it much.

Jim. Me neither.

Ella. See you going to school tomorrow?

Jim. Sure.

Ella. I gotta skip now.

Jim. Me too.

Ella. I like you, Jim.

Jim. I like you.

Ella. Don't forget.

Jim. Don't you.

Ella. Good-bye.

Jim. So long. (*They run, then turn*)

Ella. Don't forget.

Jim. I won't, you bet.

Ella. Here!

(Ella *kisses her hand at him, then runs off in frantic embarrassment*)

Jim (*overcome*) Gee! (*Runs off*)

ANNE OF GREEN GABLES

By Alice Chadwicke
From the novel by L. M. Montgomery

Anne Shirley, an imaginative, vivacious teenage girl, has come from an orphanage to live with Marilla Cuthbert and her brother, Matthew, at Green Gables. After many mishaps, Anne at last finds a real friend in Diana Barry.

Scene—*The Cuthberts' sitting-room, Green Gables, Avonlea.*

Time—1906.

Diana (*outside of the door* R; *loudly*) Anne—yoo hoo—oh, Anne where are you?

Anne (*jumping up breathlessly*) There's Diana now. (*She rushes over to the* R *door and opens same*) Come on in, Diana.

(Diana *enters* R. *She wears a light-coloured frock with wide puffed sleeves. Her skirt has been lengthened, too, and her hair has been "put up", The two girls greet each other affectionately, then come down* C, Anne R. *of Diana*)

Diana (*eagerly*) What were you doing just now, Anne?

Anne (*rushing over to the table* RC *and picking up her foolscap pad*) I'm just finishing my latest story. I do hope Miss Stacy will like it.

Diana (*bewildered*) Finishing it? Why, I haven't even started mine. I never know what to write about. (*Crosses to sofa* LC *and sits*)

Anne (*crossing to* R *of sofa; enthusiastically*) Why, it's as easy as wink.

Diana (*complainingly*) It's easy for you because you have an imagination. What would you do if you'd been born without one? What's the name of your story?

Anne (*the foolscap pad in her hand*) It's called "The Jealous Rival; or, In Death Divided". I read it to Marilla, that is, all she would listen to, and she said it was stuff and nonsense.

Diana (*agog with curiosity*) What's the story about?

Anne (*with extreme seriousness*) It's very sad, Diana. I cried like a child when I wrote it. It's all about two beautiful maidens called Cordelia Montmorency and Geraldine Seymour who lived in the same village and were devotedly attached to each other. Cordelia was a regal brunette with a coronet of midnight hair and dusky flashing eyes. Geraldine was a queenly blonde with hair like spun gold and *velvety purple* eyes.

Diana (*dubiously*) I never saw anybody with purple eyes

Anne (*facing Diana*) Neither did I. I just imagined them I wanted

9

something that wasn't common, something *instinctive*. Geraldine had an alabaster brow, too. I've found out what an alabaster brow is. That's one reason I don't mind having birthdays once every year. You know so much more on each *preceding* birthday.

DIANA. Don't you mean succeeding, Anne?

ANNE (*happily*) There, you see, now you're starting to use your imagination.

DIANA (*doubtfully*) Well, what became of Geraldine and Cordelia?

ANNE (*glancing at her foolscap pad*) They grew in beauty side by side until they were sixteen. Then Bertram De Vere came to their native village and fell in love with the fair Geraldine. Bertram proposed to her and that took up a whole page. I made it very romantic. I rewrote that speech five times and I look upon it as my masterpiece. So they became engaged, but then, alas, shadows began to darken over their path.

DIANA (*eagerly*) What sort of shadows?

ANNE (*dramatically*) Cordelia was secretly in love with Bertram herself and when she heard they were engaged she vowed that Geraldine should never wed him. But she pretended to be Geraldine's friend just the same though all her love had turned to hate.

DIANA (*tremendously impressed*) How awful! What happened?

ANNE (*impressively*) One evening they were standing on the bridge over a turbulent stream and Cordelia, thinking they were alone, pushed Geraldine over the brink with a wild, mocking, "Ha! Ha! Ha!" But Bertram saw it all and he plunged immediately into the current, shouting, "Fear not, I shall save thee, my peerless Geraldine!"

DIANA (*jumping up, excitedly*) And did he?

ANNE (*sorrowfully*) Alas, no! He had forgotten to bring his water wings and he couldn't swim so they were both drowned, clasped in each other's arms.

DIANA (*tearfully*) Oh, I don't like that. It's too sad.

ANNE (*enthusiastically*) But it's ever so much more romantic this way, Diana. It's better to wind up a story with a funeral than with a wedding. As for Cordelia, I'm just finishing up on her now. She went insane with remorse and was shut up in a lunatic asylum. I think that will be a poetical retribution for her crime.

DIANA (*sighing deeply*) How perfectly lovely. Oh, I do wish I had your imagination, Anne.

ANNE (*gravely*) It gets me into a lot of trouble at times. And upon certain occasions it makes me as blue as can be. When I think of the examinations at the end of the coming term, and how disappointed Matthew and Marilla will be if I fail . . .

DIANA (*breaking in loyally*) But you can't fail. Everybody in school says that you'll head the class unless Gil . . .

ANNE (*interrupting her angrily*) Diana, you ought to know better than to mention his name to me. If Gil—I mean, a certain boy, thinks he can annoy me by trying to get ahead of me in class, he's just got another think coming. (*She tosses her head disdainfully*)

BEAUTY AND THE BEAST

By Nicholas Stuart Gray

Beauty's visit home is drawing to a close and she must return to the Beast. Her twin sisters are jealous and tearful before her departure.

SCENE—*Beauty's bedroom in her father's house.*

Period—*1840.*

> JESSAMINE *and* JONQUILINE *are sitting side by side on the bed. They look very sad, and sniff occasionally. After a few moments* JESSAMINE *rubs her nose with the back of her hand.*

JESSAMINE. If we weren't quite so silly, we could think of the right things to say that would keep her here with us.

JONQUILINE. But we can't. We've said everything we can think of. We've begged and begged her to stay . . . and oh, how we've cried.

JESSAMINE. She has made up her mind.

JONQUILINE. And she's going to leave us, again.

JESSAMINE. And go back to that horrid Beast, and his great dark castle. She can't like the Beast as much as she likes us.

JONQUILINE. How could she?

JESSAMINE. She's sorry for him. All this week she has been worrying about him . . . and wondering if he is having proper meals, and staying out at night in the forest. She's *very* sorry for him.

JONQUILINE. I'm a bit sorry for him too, but not very much. Not if he takes Beauty away from us.

JESSAMINE. And he is. She's going away.

JONQUILINE. Now.

JESSAMINE. We can't stop her.

JONQUILINE. I hate the Beast!

JESSAMINE. It's not proper to hate, Jonquiline.

JONQUILINE. I don't care. I hate him.

JESSAMINE. So do I.

JONQUILINE. I wish his horrid rose would die! (*She jumps up and crosses to the rose*) It smells so sweet. Yet I wish it would die.

JESSAMINE. Then the Beast would die, also.

JONQUILINE. Then . . . then . . . oh, dear, I wish we could steal the ring.

JESSAMINE. Then Beauty couldn't go back to him, at all.

JONQUILINE. Shall we steal it? Here it is, Jessamine. (*She holds up the ring*)

JESSAMINE. That would be most improper of us, Jonquiline.

JONQUILINE. It would keep Beauty here with us.

JESSAMINE. And the Beast would die.

JONQUILINE Do you think he would . . . really?

JESSAMINE. Beauty says he would.

JONQUILINE. Then I suppose we mustn't steal it . . . and Beauty must leave us. For ever . . . (*She sobs*) . . . oh, I do hate the Beast, and his rose and this ring!

JESSAMINE. Oh, be careful!

JONQUILINE. I don't care! I don't care! I hope it's lost! I want Beauty!

JESSAMINE. But where has it gone? Jonquiline, help me . . . I can't find the ring.

JONQUILINE. I don't ca . . . what did you say?

JESSAMINE. I can *not* find the ring!

JONQUILINE. Oh, my goodness!

(*They search the floor without success for the ring*)

JESSAMINE. Oh, be quick! It's nearly ten o'clock.

JONQUILINE. There is no sign of it.

JESSAMINE. Ooh! Oh! Jonquiline . . . it must have gone down the mouse-hole.

JONQUILINE. Oh. Oh dear. Let us look.

(*They kneel on the floor and all that can be seen of them are their frilly behinds as they crouch to look down the mouse-hole in the corner*)

JESSAMINE. I can't see it.

JONQUILINE. It's dark in there.

JESSAMINE. I can't get my hand inside.

JONQUILINE. It's lost.

JESSAMINE. Completely lost.

JONQUILINF For ever.

JESSAMINE. What shall we say to Beauty? (*They both sit bolt upright on their heels*) Oh, my goodness, what will she say to us?

JESSAMINE. Jonquiline . . .

JONQUILINE. I cannot tell her. I cannot. She'll say I'm silly.

JESSAMINE. We must make up a story.

JONQUILINE. But what?

JESSAMINE. Don't cry, Jonquiline. If the ring is lost there's no use crying. And Beauty need not know just how silly you . . . we . . . have been this time.

JONQUILINE. What will you tell her?

JESSAMINE. I shall say . . . now listen, Jonquiline . . . this is quite clever of me . . . I shall say that a big bird flew through the window and carried the ring off the dressing-table, and away out into the night again. A very big bird stole it.

JONQUILINE. But that isn't true.

JESSAMINE. Well . . . it's not exactly a lie. It's a sort of excuse.

JONQUILINE. It sounds rather like a lie.

JESSAMINE. Do you want to tell Beauty that you dropped it down a mouse-hole?

JONQUILINE. No. Oh, no.

JESSAMINE. Well, you see, a mouse has really stolen it. If I say it was a bird, instead of a mouse . . . well, a bird is only a bigger mouse with wings.

JONQUILINE. It sounds better now that you have explained it.

JESSAMINE. It's just on ten o'clock.

JONQUILINE. And here comes Papa, with Beauty.

JESSAMINE. Now, do be brave, Jonquiline.

THE BLUE BIRD

By MAURICE MAETERLINCK
Translated by ALEXANDER TEIXEIRA DE MATTOS

When the woodcutter's son and daughter, Mytyl and Tyltyl, search for the Bluebird of Happiness, they visit some strange and fascinating places, but find that after all, true happiness is at home.

SCENE—*The Kindom of the Future.*

TYLTYL (*going up to the Blue Child and holding out his hand*) How do you do? . . . (*Touches child's dress*) What's that?

CHILD (*gravely touching Tyltyl's hat*) . . . And that?

TYLTYL. That? . . . That is my hat . . . Have you no hat?

CHILD. No. What is it for?

TYLTYL. It's to say, "How-do-you-do" with . . . and then for when it rains or when it's cold.

CHILD. What does that mean, when it's cold? . . .

TYLTYL. When you shiver like this: brrrr! brrr! When you blow into your hands and go like this with your arms. (*He vigorously beats his arms across his chest*)

CHILD. Is it cold on earth?

TYLTYL. Yes, sometimes, in the winter, when there is no fire . . .

CHILD. Why is there no fire?

TYLTYL. Because it's expensive and it costs money to buy wood . . .

CHILD. What is money?

TYLTYL. It's what you pay with.

CHILD. Oh . . .

TYLTYL. Some people have money and others have none. . . .

CHILD. Why not?

TYLTYL. Because they are not rich. . . . Are you rich? . . . How old are you? . . .

CHILD. I am going to be born soon. . . . I shall be born in twelve years. . . . Is it nice to be born? . . .

TYLTYL. Oh, yes, it's great fun.

CHILD. How did you manage?

TYLTYL. I can't remember. . . . It is so long ago! . . .

CHILD. They say it's lovely . . . the earth, and the live people . . .

TYLTYL. Yes. It's not bad. . . . There are birds and cakes and toys. . . . Some have them all; but those who have none can look at them . . .

14

CHILD. They tell us that the mothers stand waiting at the door. . . . They are good, aren't they?

TYLTYL. Oh, yes! . . . They are better than anything in the world! . . . and the grannies, too . . . but they die too soon. . . .

CHILD. They die? . . . What is that? . . .

TYLTYL. They go away one evening and do not come back.

CHILD. Why?

TYLTYL. How can one tell? . . . Perhaps because they feel sad. . . .

CHILD. Has yours gone?

TYLTYL. My grandmamma? . . .

CHILD. Your mamma or your grandmamma, I don't know. . . .

TYLTYL. Oh, but it's not the same thing! . . . The grannies go first; that's sad enough. . . . Mine was very kind to me. . . .

CHILD. What is the matter with your eyes? . . . Are they making pearls?

TYLTYL. No, it's not pearls. . . .

CHILD. What is it, then?

TYLTYL. It's nothing; it's all that blue, which dazzles me a little. . . .

CHILD. What is that called?

TYLTYL. What? . . .

CHILD. There, that, falling down . . .

TYLTYL. Nothing, it is a little water. . . .

CHILD. Does it come from the eyes? . . .

TYLTYL. Yes, sometimes, when one cries. . . .

CHILD. What does that mean, crying? . . .

TYLTYL. I have not been crying; it is the fault of that blue. . . . But if I had cried it would be the same thing . . .

CHILD. Does one often cry?

TYLTYL. Not little boys but little girls do. . . . Don't you cry here?

CHILD. No; I don't know how. . . .

TYLTYL. Well, you will learn. . . . What are you playing with, those great blue wings?

CHILD. These? . . . That's for the invention that I shall make on earth.

TYLTYL. What invention? . . . Have you invented something?

CHILD. Why yes, haven't you heard? When I am on earth I shall have to invent the thing that gives happiness. . . .

TYLTYL. Is it good to eat? . . . Does it make a noise?

CHILD. No. You hear nothing.

TYLTYL. That's a pity. . . .

CHILD. I work at it every day. . . . It is almost finished. . . . Would you like to see it? . . .

TYLTYL. Very much. . . . Where is it?

CHILD. There . . . you can see it from here between those two columns. . . .

THE BLUE BIRD

Scene—*The Woodcutter's Cottage.*

Mytyl *and* Tyltyl *are asleep. Enter* Mummy Tyl.

Mummy Tyl (*in a cheerfully scolding voice*) Up, come, get up, you little lazy bones! . . . Aren't you ashamed of yourselves? . . . It has struck eight and the sun is high above the trees! . . . Lord, how they sleep, how they sleep! . . . (*Kisses them*) They are quite rosy. . . . Tyltyl smells of lavender and Mytyl of lilies of the valley. . . . (*Kisses them again*) What sweet things children are! . . . Still, they can't go on sleeping till midday. . . . I mustn't let them grow up idle. . . . And besides I've heard that it's not very healthy. . . . (*She shakes Tyltyl*) Wake up, wake up, Tyltyl. . . .

Tyltyl (*waking up*) What? . . . Light? . . . Where is she? . . . No, no, don't go away. . . .

Mummy Tyl. Light? . . . Why, of course it's light. . . . Has been for ever so long. . . . It's as bright as noonday, though the shutters are closed. . . . Wait a bit till I open them. (*She pushes back the shutters, dazzling sunlight*) There! See! . . . What's the matter with you? . . . You look quite blinded. . . .

Tyltyl (*rubbing his eyes*) Mummy, Mummy . . . it's you! . . .

Mummy Tyl. Why, of course it's I. . . . Who did you think it was? . . .

Tyltyl. It's you. . . . Yes, yes, it's you! . . .

Mummy Tyl. Yes, yes, it's I. . . . I haven't changed my face since last night. . . . Why do you stare at me in that wonder-struck way? . . . Is my nose turned upside down by any chance?

Tyltyl. Oh, how nice it is to see you again! . . . It's so long, —so long ago! . . . I must kiss you at once. . . . Again! Again! And how comfortable my bed is . . . I am back at home!

Mummy Tyl. What's the matter? Why don't you wake up? . . . Don't tell me you're ill. . . . Let me see, show me your tongue. . . . Come, get up and dress. . . .

Tyltyl. Hallo! . . . I've got my shirt on.

Mummy Tyl. Of course you have. . . . Put on your breeches and your little jacket. . . . There they are on the chair. . . .

Tyltyl. Is that what I did on the journey?

Mummy Tyl. What journey?

Tyltyl. Why, last year. . . .

Mummy Tyl. Last year? . . .

Tyltyl. Why, yes, at Christmas, when I went away. . . .

Mummy Tyl. When you went away? . . . You haven't left the

16

room. . . . I put you to bed last night and here you are this morning.
. . . Have you dreamed all that?

TYLTYL. But you don't understand! . . . It was last year, when I
went away with Mytyl, the Fairy, Light, how nice Light is! . . .
Bread, Sugar, Water, Fire: they did nothing but quarrel! . . . You're
not angry with me? . . . Did you feel very sad? And what did daddy
say? . . . I could not refuse. . . . I left a note to explain. . . .

MUMMY TYL. What are you talking about? For sure, either you're
ill, or else you're still asleep. . . . (*She gives him a friendly shake*) There,
wake up. . . . There, is that better? . . .

TYLTYL. But, Mummy, I assure you, it's you that's still asleep. . . .

MUMMY TYL. What? Still asleep am I? . . . Why, I've been up
since six o'clock. . . . I've finished all the cleaning and lit the fire. . . .

TYLTYL. But ask Mytyl if it's not true. . . . Oh, we have had such
adventures! . . .

MUMMY TYL. Why, Mytyl? . . . What do you mean?

TYLTYL. She was with me. . . . We saw Grandad and Granny. . . .

MUMMY TYL (*more and more bewildered*) Grandad and Granny? . . .

TYLTYL. Yes, in the Land of Memory. . . . It was on our way. . . .
They are dead, but they are quite well. . . . Granny made us a lovely
plum tart. . . . And then the little brothers—Robert, Jean and his
top . . . and Madeleine and Pierette and Pauline and Riquette,
too. . . . And Pauline still has a pimple on her nose!

MUMMY TYL. Have you found the key of the cupboard where
Daddy hides his brandy bottle?

TYLTYL. Does Daddy hide a brandy bottle?

MUMMY TYL. Certainly. One has to hide everything when one
has little meddlesome good-for-nothings like you. . . . But come,
out with it . . . confess that you took it. . . . I would rather it was
that. . . . I shan't tell Daddy. . . . I shan't beat you. . . .

TYLTYL. But, Mummy, I don't know where it is. . . .

MUMMY TYL. Just walk in front of me so that I may see if you can
walk straight. . . .

(TYLTYL *does so*)

No, it's not that. . . . Dear Heaven, what is the matter with you?
(*Suddenly mad with alarm, she calls out*) Daddy Tyl! . . . Come quick!
The children are ill!

CIRCUS BOY

By Michael Redgrave

Janet Poddington has run away to join the gypsies and greets Ludo, an attractive fifteen-year-old gypsy boy, and his chimpanzee, Sophie.

SCENE—*Behind the scenes at a circus.*

TIME—*The present.*

LUDO. Sophie, what's the matter with you today? You won't let me have a moment's peace. Are you hungry?

(SOPHIE *shakes her head*)

Well, what's the matter? Ill?

(SOPHIE *shakes her head*)

If you can't tell me what it is I can't help you. I caught sight of you when I was up on the wire for my first act. I thought you'd gone mad. Did you want me to fall off?

(SOPHIE *shakes her head*)

You looked as if you thought I was *going* to.

(SOPHIE *nods violently*)

So you thought I was going to. You're a silly old woman, Sophie. I won't fall.

(JANET *enters* R)

JANET. Hullo.
LUDO. Hullo—thought they sent you home.
JANET. They did, only I didn't go. I gave the chauffeur the slip and came back. I saw a bit of the circus.
LUDO. Well, you're missing it in here.
JANET. I most wanted to see you.
LUDO. Well, here I am.
JANET. It's a wonder you are.
LUDO (*proudly*) Did you think I'd fall?
JANET. No, I knew you'd be all right.
LUDO. Right as rain, thank you. Where are all your fine friends?
JANET. Oh, sitting in there. I didn't let them see me. Bobo let me in at the back of the cheap seats. (*She crosses and sits beside Ludo*)

(SOPHIE *rises and plays with Janet's hair*)

LUDO. Sophie! Manners!

18

(SOPHIE *gives Ludo a sulky look and crouches down*)

Is that a way to behave? (*To Janet*) She let you touch her. That
was brave of you, for a girl.

JANET. I don't see why girls shouldn't be just as brave as boys.

LUDO. Nor do I, but they aren't.

JANET. They are, sometimes.

LUDO. Sometimes isn't always.

JANET (*changing the subject*) How did you know she wouldn't hurt me?

LUDO. I just knew.

JANET. But how?

LUDO. It's a secret.

JANET. Tell me.

LUDO. Isn't it enough that she didn't hurt you?

JANET. If there's a secret about why she likes me I ought to know.

LUDO. You'd better ask her. I can't tell you, it's an important
secret.

JANET. Please tell me.

LUDO. You're like all girls. You just want what you can't get.
You think you can walk in here and worm things out of people just
by asking. But mine are important secrets, and secrets are only
important if they're kept.

JANET. Oh, all right, then.

LUDO. You're not bad, for a girl. You're the only one I know
who'd have dared to walk up to Sophie like that. And there's not
many girls would run away like you did. But it doesn't alter facts.
You belong to the ordinary people. I'm a gypsy, my secrets are
gypsy secrets.

JANET. But that's just it. I want to be a gypsy, too.

LUDO. You want to be a Romany, a gypsy?

JANET. Yes. That's why I ran away. I love the gypsies.

LUDO (*suspiciously*) Do you know any?

JANET. No, but I'd love to live the way you live. I'd like to be all
free and in the open air. To have music, and noise and excitement,
and never have to go to school.

LUDO. How old are you?

JANET. Thirteen. Why?

LUDO. Then gypsy or no gypsy, you've got another year at school.

JANET. Do gypsies go to school?

LUDO. 'Course they do, but it's a waste of time. Gypsies don't
need that sort of knowledge. They've got their own sort. It's just
as important.

JANET. Yes: making fires, and cooking, and getting fresh water
and things.

LUDO. Yes, and feeding animals, and nursing them, and helping
them to be born, and sometimes having to kill them. Oh, thousands
of things. The trouble is, people seem to think everybody ought to
live the same way.

JANET. Yes, I know. It's like that at Poddington. That's why I left. That's why I'm going to be a gypsy. You're going to help me, aren't you?

LUDO. You're probably much better off in the castle.

JANET (*disappointed*) You know, anybody else would have said, "I'd love to help you."

LUDO. Why?

JANET. I don't know. Out of politeness, I suppose.

LUDO. But I don't see why I should help you. You'd be horribly in the way. Why would it be polite to pretend you wouldn't? Anyway, I'm not anyone else, I'm Ludo, I'm a gypsy. I can do things other people can't.

JANET. You're jolly conceited, if you ask me.

LUDO. I don't ask you.

JANET. It's conceit, all the same.

LUDO. It's the truth. I'd rather be what I am than anybody else. I can ride, I can shoot. I know when it's going to be fine and when it's going to rain, I can play a pipe, I can light a fire, I'm the only one who can keep Sophie tame. Hundreds of things I can do—and best of all I can dance on the high wire.

JANET (*thrilled in spite of herself*) What's that?

LUDO. It's my second act. The first one, the one you saw, that's nothing. That was only walking. Next time, I dance and play the pipe at the same time.

JANET. How thrilling!

LUDO (*with a gesture*) Then I jump, down, down, down, into a tiny net, the size of a bed.

JANET. Why don't you have a great big net? It'd be easier.

LUDO. I don't want it easy, stupid. I want it hard.

JANET (*ignoring the insult*) But if you missed—you'd be killed.

LUDO. I don't miss. That's the whole point.

JANET (*gazing at him with intense admiration*) I see.

LUDO. I don't know how other kids can bear all the things they have to do. Living in awful houses, being told to do things, having to let their parents know where they've been, and what they're doing.

JANET. That's all right, if you've got a nice home and nice parents, you know.

LUDO. Are yours nice?

JANET. I haven't got any.

LUDO. No home?

JANET. No.

LUDO. Nor parents?

JANET. Not any more.

LUDO. Is that why you live at Poddington what-not?

JANET. Mm!

LUDO. And don't you like it?

JANET. I loathe it.

LUDO. Well, if you don't like it, don't do it.

JANET. I don't want to. Only you said I'd be in the way here.

LUDO. If you really wanted to come, you wouldn't mind what anyone said. You'd just come.

EMIL AND THE DETECTIVES

Adapted by CYRUS BROOKS
From the novel by ERIC KÄESTNER

This play is adapted from the German novel, written in 1929.

EMIL *is a small boy, uncomfortably dressed in his best suit.*
MRS TITCHBURN, *his mother, is a hard-working widow.*

SCENE—*Gothersham Railway Station.*

TIME—*1930's.*

MOTHER. Now listen, Emil—don't let anyone know you've got all that money in your pocket.

EMIL (*feels in his breast-pocket*) I shall tell every soul I meet.

MOTHER. Don't be so cheeky when you speak to your mother! Have you still got it safe?

(*They sit on the seat*)

EMIL (*on* R *of his mother; again feels in breast-pocket*) Yes, Mrs Titchburn.

MOTHER. Where did you put your ticket?

EMIL. Here! All aboard for London town!

MOTHER. And what are you going to say to Granny?

EMIL (*bows and talks to bunch of flowers as though it were his grandmother*) Dear Granny—then I expect she'll give me a kiss (*kisses flowers*)—dear Granny, here's seven pounds. (*Feels in his breast-pocket*) Six pounds are for you. With love from your daughter Maggie in Gothersham. (*He points to his Mother*) And please don't be cross with her for not sending you anything last month, because we were awful hard up. So this time I've brought it myself. Here you are! And then I expect she'll give me another kiss. (*Kisses flowers*)

MOTHER. And what are you going to do with the other pound, you young scamp?

EMIL. First I've got to pay my fare back home. That will be seven and tenpence. And that will leave—er—leave—er—twelve and tuppence to pay for my meals if we go out anywhere. It's always a good thing to have a few shillings in your pocket, you never know what's going to happen. (*He feels in his breast-pocket*) Waiter, bill, please! We had half a yard of pork sausages and mashed potatoes with raspberry jam.

MOTHER (*puts her hand over his mouth*) Haven't you had enough dinner?

22

(EMIL *pats his tummy*)

Here are three sandwiches to eat in the train. (*She puts them on the suitcase*)

EMIL. I shall burst. I say, have you got your platform ticket?

MOTHER. Yes, yes, you needn't worry about me.

EMIL. But I do worry about you. Don't work too hard, Mummie. And mind you have proper meals.

(MOTHER *strokes his shoulder*)

Mrs Crump is coming for a shampoo, isn't she?

MOTHER. Yes, at two sharp. And at half-past four Miss Peters is coming to have her hair done. She's off to a dance at the drill-hall tonight.

EMIL. I wish you'd got an electric hair-dryer. It's such hard work for you rubbing their heads.

MOTHER. A bit of exercise does me good.

EMIL. Are you sure you've kept enough money? I don't need a whole pound, and you know you could get some . . .

MOTHER. Will you do as you're bid?

(POLICE-SERGEANT *enters* L)

I've got plenty. Besides, I shall earn a few shillings this afternoon.

(EMIL *salutes and stands to attention.* POLICE-SERGEANT FIELD *comes up behind them*)

FIELD. Hello, young lad, I suppose you are off to Australia?

(EMIL *turns round with a start*)

MOTHER (*rising*) Afternoon, Sergeant. No, Emil's going to London for a week. To stay with his Granny.

FIELD. What, all by himself?

MOTHER. His granny's going to meet him at Charing Cross Station with his little cousin. They'll be waiting by the bookstall.

FIELD. Ever been to London before?

(EMIL *shakes his head*)

Ho-ho! He'll like London all right. There's plenty there to keep a youngster occupied. We took the Bowling Club up two years ago. Awful noisy place! How's business, Mrs Titchburn?

MOTHER. Thank you, Sergeant, we mustn't grumble.

FIELD. Well, good day to you. (*Crosses* R) Have a good time, Emil, and mind you don't get up to any monkey-tricks. (*Shakes his finger with mock severity*) There's a policeman at every street-corner in London.

(EMIL *touches his cap*, FIELD *salutes and walks off*)

EMIL (*takes a deep breath, sits* C) I'm glad he's gone. I thought he was going to arrest me.

MOTHER (*sits* R *of Emil*) Arrest you?

EMIL. Yes.

MOTHER. But what for?

EMIL. Promise you won't split! Promise!

MOTHER.　　　See this wet, see this dry?
　　　　　　　Cut my throat if I ever tell a lie.

EMIL. Then I'll tell you. You know the statue of the first Lord Gothersham in the recreation grounds—the chap with his nose all skew-wiff? When we came out of gym the other day we put a mouldy old hat on his head.

MOTHER. Well!

EMIL. They shoved me up because I'm good at drawing, and I had some chalk, and I gave the statue a red nose and a black moustache. And while I was up there, Sergeant Field came round the corner from the market. We didn't half run. But I'm sure he saw who it was. Suppose he's said "Emil Titchburn, hands up! I arrest you in the name of the law!"

MOTHER. Of course he wouldn't.

EMIL. But didn't you notice how he looked at me, and what he said about me not getting up to monkey-tricks?

(*Train noise off stage*)

MOTHER. All your fancy! Here's the train coming.

EMIL AND THE DETECTIVES

EMIL *is now tired and discouraged.*

GUS, *Emil's age, is the leader of a street gang.*

SCENE—*Outside a teashop.*

EMIL *springs up with a start and looks round.*

GUS (*laughs*) Now, you, don't jump out of your skin!

EMIL. I just heard a car.

GUS. You didn't hear no car.

EMIL. Yes, I did. What was it hooting, then?

GUS. Me, of course. You don't live round about Fleet Street, or you'd know I carry a hooter in my trouser-pocket. (*He shows the hooter proudly*) I'm as well-known in Fleet Street as Lord Beaverbrook.

EMIL (*still watching teashop door*) I live in Gothersham. I've only just come from London Bridge Station.

GUS. Gothersham? . . . That explains why you've got such a rum-looking suit on.

EMIL. Take that back, or I'll knock your block off!

GUS. Coo! You haven't half got a temper. Just like that, eh? It's too hot for scrapping, still, if you're keen on it . . .

EMIL (*watching teashop door*) Let's leave it till later. I haven't got time for it now.

GUS. You seem to have heaps of time. Standing there with an old bag and a bunch of daisies, playing hide and seek with yourself.

EMIL. I'm watching a thief.

GUS. What? Did I hear you say "thief"? Who's he robbed?

EMIL (*almost proudly*) Me! In the train. While I was asleep. Seven pounds! I was bringing it for my grandmother. She lives here in London. He must have sneaked along to another compartment. Then he got out at London Bridge and I followed him. You bet your life!

GUS. Coo, and what then?

EMIL. He got on a bus. He went upstairs and I went inside, and when we got here, he got out, so I got out too.

GUS. Yes—go on! (*In his enthusiasm he comes closer and closer to* EMIL)

EMIL (*taking him by the arm and leading him to the teashop door*) There he is, just by the corner of the counter. The man with the bowler hat. See him?

GUS. Sure! The one with the black blob on his nob.

EMIL. He looks pretty well pleased with himself, too, the swine!

25

Gus. Coo, if that don't beat everything. Just like at the pictures. What are you going to do with him?

Emil. Darned if I know. Stick to him. What else can I do?

Gus. And when you've got him I suppose you'll say, "Please give me back my money, kind sir!" And then he'll say, "Certainly, my good lad, here it is. I promise never to do such a thing again." Not likely! Why don't you tell that copper? He'll run him in.

Emil. I can't. You see, I've done something at home in Gothersham, and the police may be after me. If I . . .

Gus. I get you.

Emil. And my grandmother's waiting for me at Charing Cross Station. By the bookstall.

Gus. She'll soon get sick of that and hop off home. But that stuff about the thief—coo, that's a corker. That's great. What d'you say to me giving you a hand?

Emil. Oh, I wish you would. You are a brick!

Gus. Cut it out! When there's a job like this on hand, you bet I want to be in on it. My name's Gus.

Emil. Mine's Emil.

Gus. What a funny name!

Emil. Now then! (*Clenches his fist*)

Gus. Stow it! That'll keep. . . . Come on! If we stand here cooling our heels that blighter will give us the slip. (*He considers*) Have you got any money?

Emil. Not a penny.

Gus (*hooting softly*) What can we do? (*Hoots*) When he's finished his cup of tea . . . (*Hoots*)

Emil (*hesitating*) How would it be if you fetched a few of your friends?

Gus. That's a first-rate idea. Leave it to me. If I just run down the street sounding my hooter we shall have the whole gang out.

Emil. All right, Gus. But be quick, or that crook will be going and I shall have to go after him.

Gus. O.K. I'll make it nippy.

(*They go and peer through the teashop door*)

He's eating boiled eggs and things.

Emil. And he's going to pay for them with my mother's money!

AN EPISODE OF SPARROWS

By Nan MacDonald
From the novel by Rumer Godden

An unusual friendship grows between Tip Malone, a teenage boy, and Lovejoy Mason, a lonely small girl, when they try to create a garden from the rubble of a London churchyard. After many struggles with authority, the children are separated, but meet once before being sent away.

SCENE—*In the churchyard.*

TIME—*The present.*

(LOVEJOY *is sitting alone.* TIP *enters.*)

TIP. Hello.

LOVEJOY. Hello.

TIP. I'm going to the *Arethusa*. . . . I'm really going. . . . At least I hope I am. It's a training ship for the Navy.

LOVEJOY. I hope you enjoy it.

TIP. It's proper. The school's like living in a ship and we wear sailor dress.

LOVEJOY. Sailors are fashionable this year.

TIP. The St. Vincent boys gave a display in the Tattoo. I don't know if we do, but probably we will. And I'll be in it. You can come and watch.

LOVEJOY. I shan't be able to. I shall be in a Home.

TIP. My mum says you have fun in a Home. You go to school, like the others, and have nice frocks. Sometimes they give you ice-cream. . . . You got the money for the pansies?

LOVEJOY. What's the good of pansies if you can't water them?

TIP. It was your fault I couldn't come. It was you who got me caught.

LOVEJOY. You're talking just like your mum.

TIP. It's true. And you left me. You ran away.

LOVEJOY. I didn't run away! It was the garden!

TIP. Garden! Garden! All you think about's that blasted garden.

LOVEJOY. I can't water it. I've broken the cider bottle. Look, the grass has all gone brown.

TIP. 'Tisn't grass. It's mustard and cress. It's no use your bothering about the garden. There won't be any garden soon. Get that into your nut. No garden!

LOVEJOY. Why not?

TIP. Because they're going to knock it down. They've got the

27

money to build the church. The builders are going to start at once. First they'll knock the hut down, squash . . . flat!

LOVEJOY. Who told you?

TIP. Father Lambert. They'll bring a bulldozer. It'll go over the garden, like that. Over the pansies, and the pillar and the pot.

LOVEJOY. The pansies and the pillar and the pot. . . .

TIP. Yes. . . . A lot of good it's been—all that sweat!

LOVEJOY. Bloody Pigs!

TIP. Who?

LOVEJOY. Grown-ups . . . all grown-ups! (*She picks up a stone and throws it*)

TIP. Lovejoy! You've broken the statue of our Lady. . . .

THE GENTLE KNIGHT

By Willis Hall

Gon is the youngest son of King Jog and Queen Joginda. The three sons have been sent to find their fortunes, and Gon, unlike his brothers, is not interested in fighting dragons or seeking the hands of princesses. When searching in a dungeon for oil to stop his armour squeaking, he meets Albert, the dragon.

SCENE—*A Dungeon.*

The dungeon is dark and gloomy. GON, *who enters, has difficulty in finding his way about. He stumbles over something and stubs his toe.*

GON (*disparagingly*) Adventures! . . . Huh. . . . Adventures! (*He hears a noise from the darkest corner of the dungeon and turns, startled*)

GON. Who's that? Who's there? (*A pause*) I . . . I know there's someone there . . . I . . . I can hear you.

ALBERT (*from the darkness*) It's me.

GON. Who's me?

ALBERT. Me. Albert. I'm a dragon and I'm hiding in this corner.

GON. I don't believe you. Dragons don't hide in corners. Come out.

ALBERT. Shan't!

GON. Yes, you will.

ALBERT. Shan't!

GON. You'd better come out. You . . . you don't frighten me, you know. Not really.

ALBERT. I don't want to frighten anyone.

GON. Well, then, why are you hiding in a corner?

ALBERT. Because I've seen your kind before. You're a knight, aren't you?

GON. What if I am?

ALBERT. Well, then! There you are!

GON. That's no reason to hide in a corner.

ALBERT. Yes, it is. It's a jolly good reason. It's the best reason I know. If I come out of here you'll be "having at" me and . . . "Take that, you foul fiend" and . . . and all the rest of it. Oh, yes, I know you knights.

GON. No, I won't. I never "have at" anything. My brothers do. They're always "having at" things. But, honestly, not me.

ALBERT. Promise?

GON. Promise.

ALBERT. Honour bright?

GON. Honour bright.

29

ALBERT. Cross your heart?

GON. If you like.

ALBERT. I would like to come out. Really I would. It's awfully damp in this corner. And I think there's a spider, or something, crawling down my neck. (*He wheezes unhappily*)

GON. Well, you needn't be afraid of me. I won't touch you.

ALBERT (*taking a tentative step out of the darkness*) Thank you very much. (*He crosses a little closer to Gon*) But I warn you, if you so much as reach for your sword I'll be back in that corner before you can say "have at you".

GON. It's a poor kind of dragon that hides in corners.

ALBERT. Yes. That may be true. But at least it's a live dragon. And that's more than I'd be if I went about ravaging the country-side and . . . and all that kind of thing.

GON. How did you get down here in the first place?

ALBERT. Ah! Now, that's a story and a half, that is. They locked me up down here.

GON. Who did?

ALBERT. They did. The princesses. Who do you think?

GON. I don't believe it!

ALBERT. It's true all right. I've been locked away down here for as long as I can remember.

GON. Why?

ALBERT. Well, you see, the trouble with me is that I'm a kind of dragon in the family cupboard. They're ashamed of me. That's what they are.

GON. But why?

ALBERT. Promise not to laugh?

GON. Promise.

ALBERT. It's because I wheeze.

GON. You what?

ALBERT. Wheeze. Yes, I can't snort like a real dragon. I only wheeze. Listen. (*He wheezes*)

GON. That's nothing to be ashamed of. It's quite a pleasant wheeze.

ALBERT. Do you think so?

GON. Sure of it.

ALBERT. I can't breathe fire either. Only a kind of damp smoke, and not very much of that. But it's awfully jolly, really. Rather like an engine. Watch. (*He opens his mouth and breathes out heavily*) There! Did you see that?

GON. I don't think so.

ALBERT (*disappointed*) Oh.

GON. Well, perhaps just a little bit. It's very clever.

ALBERT. And you don't think my wheeze is anything to laugh about?

GON. Not at all. As a matter of fact, I squeak.

ALBERT. Do you?

GON. Yes, it's my armour. Listen. (*He squeaks*) My brothers are always laughing at me.

ALBERT. I know just how you feel. What's your name?

GON. Gon. Prince Gon. My brothers are called Gawain and Gawain.

ALBERT. I like you, Gon. But I don't think I would like your brothers. Not if they "have at" things.

GON. No. I'm not very fond of them myself. But you needn't worry about them. Not at the moment. They're far too busy with the princesses to start looking for dragons.

ALBERT. That's all right then. Those girls could keep any knight occupied.

GON. Albert?

ALBERT. Yes?

GON. Why don't you escape?

ALBERT. Escape?

GON. Yes. You know—run away.

ALBERT. Oh, I couldn't do that. (*A pause*) Could I?

GON. Why not?

ALBERT. Nowhere to go. There isn't a dragon in these parts that would have anything to do with me. Not with my wheeze, they wouldn't. It makes it very lonely—having a wheeze.

GON. But—supposing I came with you?

ALBERT. You?

GON. Yes. Why not?

ALBERT. Well, because I'm a dragon and you're a knight, that's why. I mean, we just couldn't be seen out together. (*He pauses*) Would you really come with me?

GON. I'd love to. I've had more than enough of adventures and pricesses and this armour and—oh—everything. I'd be very glad to come with you, Albert.

ALBERT. When?

GON. Right now. Today. This minute.

ALBERT (*a little afraid at the prospect*) Now?

GON. If we're going to do it, it's the best time. The princesses wouldn't notice you were missing. The door's open. Gawain and Gawain are much too busy to think about me.

ALBERT. You needn't worry about your brothers. Not if I know anything about those two princesses. The whole castle could come tumbling down and they wouldn't notice. Not once those girls start talking. Oh, yes, let's. It must be wonderful in the fields now. The grass so tall and the birds singing. Once, they let me out. On a long lead. And I found a thrush's nest, with three eggs . . . and a rabbit hole and . . . and all kinds of things. (*He wheezes happily*)

GON. All right. Let's slip out now. Let's go right away, Albert.

ALBERT. Come along, then. I know a place where we can find blackberries. . . . Here, take my claw.

And, squeaking and wheezing, hand in hand, GON *and the dragon scamper off stage. The* LIGHTS *fade.*

THE GLASS SLIPPER

By Eleanor and Herbert Farjeon

When the Prince meets Cinderella, he believes her to be the Princess of Nowhere.

Scene—*At the Ball.*

Prince (*moving up stage and calling her*) Princess!

(*The* Princess *turns. The* Prince *approaches and kisses her hand*)

Cinderella. Oh!
Prince. What is the matter?
Cinderella. Nobody has ever done that before. (*Putting out her hand*) Would you do it again?

(*He does so. Both are* c)

How strange it all is!
Prince. They do not kiss hands in Nowhere?
Cinderella. No. Yes. Do they? I—can't remember.
Prince. You have been so long absent from your native land?
Cinderella. Yes. No. Have I? How stupid you must think me!
Prince. I think you . . .
Cinderella. What?
Prince. I cannot tell you so soon.
Cinderella (*out front*) In Nowhere we tell at once.
Prince. Tell, then.
Cinderella (*looking at him*) I—I think—I think you . . .
Prince. Well?
Cinderella (*looking down*) I can't either . . . What a magnificent room! (*She moves down* R, *then across to* L)
Prince. I suppose so.
Cinderella (*facing him*) Don't you love it?
Prince. I think I am a little tired of it.
Cinderella. I couldn't ever grow tired of it—unless I had to clean it.
Prince. Clean it? You!
Cinderella. I mean—you see—in Nowhere—we *do* sometimes clean things ourselves. Oh, yes, indeed.
Prince. Whatever for?
Cinderella (*airily*) Different countries, different customs. It never hurts anybody to know what scouring and scrubbing are. . . . (*Looking around*) Your poor servants!

32

PRINCE. Why?

CINDERELLA. Just think of polishing these acres of floors! (*crossing to the throne*) Just think of shining up the throne every morning before they come down! And the dusting! (*Examining*) I thought so! Dust under the throne!

PRINCE (*crossing to her*) It doesn't matter.

CINDERELLA. It does matter.

PRINCE (*taking her arm and moving* L) Don't let's talk about dusting. Tell me about Nowhere. Tell me all about your castles. Describe them to me. Have you many castles?

CINDERELLA. I—we don't have castles in Nowhere.

PRINCE. What an unusual country! Then tell me about your acrobats. Have you good acrobats in Nowhere?

CINDERELLA. We don't have acrobats.

PRINCE. No acrobats?

CINDERELLA. No ... (*Tossing her head*) We don't approve of them. (*She sits on the downstage stool,* L)

PRINCE (*sitting on the upstage stool*) I suppose it is a point of view. How many horses do you keep?

CINDERELLA. We don't keep horses. (*With dignity*) But we have lots and lots of mice.

PRINCE. How charming! I will keep mice, too. I am glad you are fond of animals. And are you fond of art? People in our position should patronize art, don't you think? Have you a fine gallery? Do you like pictures?

CINDERELLA. Yes, yes, I do, I do ... I intend to get some.

PRINCE. We have many fine pictures. (*Rising, taking her hand and leading her up stage* R) Look. (*Pointing off*) That is a picture of my great-great-grandmother.

CINDERELLA. What lovely green hair!

PRINCE. Yes, she was a water-nymph. In one of the best rivers, of course. And this (*leading her across*) is my grand-grand-great-uncle. (*He points off* L)

CINDERELLA. You aren't very like him.

PRINCE. No.

CINDERELLA. I'm glad.

PRINCE. He couldn't help having two noses. He offended a witch.

(CINDERELLA *turns to the Prince*)

CINDERELLA. Poor man.

PRINCE. Poor man.

BOTH. Poor man.

(*A little pause*)

CINDERELLA. What did he do to offend the witch?

PRINCE (*taking her hand*) He cut off her nose.

CINDERELLA. Poor witch.

PRINCE. Poor witch.

(*They stand close together, shoulder to shoulder. There is another little pause*)

BOTH. Poor witch.

(*They move down stage four paces, then stop. She sighs. Again there is a pause*)

CINDERELLA (*breaking away*) What is the time?
PRINCE. Who cares?
CINDERELLA. What *is* the time?
PRINCE. Ten minutes past eleven.
CINDERELLA. Oh. (*She shuts her eyes*) How many seconds is fifty minutes?
PRINCE. Three thousand—why?
CINDERELLA. Three thousand—three thousand.
PRINCE. Yes, and time flies. I must attend to my guests.
CINDERELLA. Must you?
PRINCE. I must. (*Turning up stage*) Herald!

(*Enter* HERALD *up* L)

HERALD. Your Royal Highness?
PRINCE. It is ten minutes past eleven. Summon the ladies. Let the dancing begin.
HERALD. So be it. The ladies shall be summoned.

(*Exit* HERALD. *His voice is heard calling* "Ladies, attend!" *Herald-and Lady-noises off all through the following*)

CINDERELLA (*crossing to the throne*) The ladies are very accomplished?
PRINCE (*following*) Accomplished? No doubt, in their way.
CINDERELLA. The ladies will have been taught dancing?
PRINCE. Presumably.
CINDERELLA. We are not taught dancing in Nowhere. (*She takes two steps back*)
PRINCE (*following her*) I am sure you have no need to be.
CINDERELLA. We do not dance very well in Nowhere. (*She takes two more steps back*)
PRINCE (*following her*) You are too modest.
CINDERELLA. I'm not, I'm not. (*She takes one step back*)
PRINCE. Nevertheless, you will be my partner?
CINDERELLA. Yes. I will be your partner. Will you do something for me? (*She takes a step forward*)
PRINCE. Anything you ask.
CINDERELLA (*holding out her hand*) Kiss my hand again.

(*The* PRINCE *kisses it*)

Thank you.

HANSEL AND GRETEL

By Lillian and Robert Masters

Hansel and Gretel, two young children, have been left in the wood by their father.

Scene—*Deep in the wood.*

Gretel (*looking after him*) Poor Father. He loves us so much, and he would be unhappy without us.

Hansel. Yes. He didn't want to leave us here. He never would have thought of it except for Stepmother.

Gretel. He told us good-bye as if he should never see us again.

Hansel. But how happy he'll be to find us at home in the morning.

Gretel. Oh, yes. He will laugh and cry again with joy. Hansel, it was clever of you to mark the way with breadcrumbs so we could find our way back to him. Come on, let's hurry. (*She skips towards the edge to the* R)

Hansel. Wait. We must let him get home first so Stepmother will know that he really left us as she made him promise to do.

Gretel (*comes back to Hansel*) Yes, of course. Then she can't be angry with him when we return.

Hansel (*pointing behind the stump at* L) Look, there are wild strawberries. Shall we have a feast?

Gretel. What lovely ones! And so good. (*She pops one into her mouth*)

Hansel. Sit down and I'll fill your lap.

Gretel (*sits on the stump down* L) All right. And we shall take my apronful home to Father.

Hansel. Here are some big ones.

Gretel. You know, Hansel, I'm not a bit frightened now, even though this is a gloomy place.

Hansel. This experience will make a man of us, Gretel, I mean of me.

(*They laugh*)

Gretel. Look, I've made a wreath of strawberry leaves!

Hansel. Here. (*He puts it on her head*) Now you are queen of the forest. (*He bows low*) I bow to you, my strawberry queen. Accept my homage. I shall always protect my strawberry queen from jams.

Gretel. A strawberry queen in jams! (*They both laugh merrily,*

35

then she gets serious) But, Hansel, it's growing much darker. I think we should start back home.

HANSEL. Yes, the moon will be up soon and then we can easily see our trail of breadcrumbs. See, it starts from here, (*crosses* L) and then it should go this way—but . . . (*He stops suddenly, bends over and looks closely at the ground*)

GRETEL. Hansel, what is it?

(HANSEL *does not answer, but goes off* L. *She rises and calls after him,* "*Hansel*"; *crosses to* C *as he comes back*)

Hansel, tell me. Is something wrong?

(HANSEL *returns slowly.* GRETEL *runs to him*)

What is it, Hansel, tell me.

HANSEL (*meets her* C) Our trail of crumbs—the birds—they have eaten it up.

GRETEL. You mean—we can't find our way home?

(HANSEL *nods*)

(*She draws back*) Oh, Hansel!

HANSEL. I don't know the way at all!

GRETEL. Then we are really lost! Oh, Hansel, we must stop Father! (*She runs to the* L *side of the stage*) Father! Come back!

HANSEL. Father! Father!

(*They listen, but only the echo answers*)

GRETEL. He's too far gone. He can't hear us. Oh, Hansel, we're lost. We'll never find our way home! (*She cries and sits on the stump at* R)

HANSEL. Don't cry, Gretel, I'll take care of you. When morning comes perhaps we can find our way back.

GRETEL (*looking about fearfully*) Hansel, the Great Rock is deep in the forest—deeper than we've ever been—and there are wild beasts —and—and Witch Wicked!

HANSEL. Don't think about Witch Wicked. I'm trying not to.

GRETEL (*pointing off; fearfully*) Hansel, what is that glimmering there in the darkness?

HANSEL. It's only a silver birch tree.

GRETEL. But there! Grinning so at me!

HANSEL. It's only the stump of a willow!

GRETEL (*crying*) Oh, the woods are full of horrible faces and dreadful shapes!

HANSEL. No, no, you imagine all those things. (*He leads her in back of the stump*) Come, lie down on these soft leaves, and do not be frightened. (*He looks about tremblingly as they lie down*) Perhaps we can sleep, and dream that we are safe at home.

GRETEL. But I can't go to sleep, Hansel, I'm too frightened. (*Sobbing*) I want Father; I want to see Father!

HANSEL. I don't think God will let anything happen to us. We haven't been bad.

GRETEL. We shall never find our way home. Father will be so unhappy.

HANSEL. Gretel, let's pray.

(*They get to their knees, facing the audience, and sing softly the prayer song*)

> When at night I go to sleep,
> Fourteen angels watch do keep,
> Two my head are guarding,
> Two my feet are guiding,
> Two are on my right hand,
> Two are on my left hand,
> Two who warmly cover,
> Two who o'er me hover,
> To guide my steps to heaven.

(GRETEL *begins to sob. Her sobbing continues for a while, then she becomes quiet.*)

HANS, THE WITCH AND THE GOBBIN

By Alan Cullen

Hans, a medical student, seeks the help of the Queen of the Forest in finding Princess Alicia's lost memory.

Scene—*The Grotto of the Queen of the Forest.*

Queen. The Princess Alicia is safe enough for the moment, Hans.

Hans (*moving* c) How did you know I was thinking of her?

Queen. The Queen of the Forest knows everything. The trees watch and the grass listens, and the wind tells me what they hear— (*she sits on the throne*) and what they see.

Hans. Were those the voices I heard?

Queen. Those were the voices of the Grotto. They are meaningless.

Hans. They seemed to be telling me to turn back, to run away.

Queen. There is no turning back now, Hans, and no running away. If you did not need help you should not have come.

Hans (*kneeling*) I do need your help.

Queen. What do you want of me? Fame? Wealth? Honour?

Hans. I want nothing for myself.

Queen (*mockingly*) Noble and unselfish Hans. For whom, then?

Hans. For—for someone who is very near to me. For the Princess Alicia.

Queen. My help is rarely given, and not given easily. (*She rises*) You must be prepared to pay for it. (*She moves a little down* LC)

Hans (*rising*) I am a poor man, Your Majesty. But anything I can give I will give willingly to see the Princess restored to her former self.

Queen. Even your life, Hans? Would you give your life?

Hans. If it were the only thing I could give, yes, I would.

Queen. It may come to that; because those who ask for my help must first risk their lives to obtain it. (*She moves down* LC) Look around you. Those faces of stone were once the faces of living men. They asked for my help, but they failed in the tasks I set them to earn it.

(Hans *moves up* L, *looks at the statues, crosses and looks at the statues* R, *then turns to look at the Queen*)

Now you know the risk—do you still ask for my help?

Hans. I still ask it.

Queen. Very well. It is a simple task. If you can answer one question I shall put to you, and answer it correctly, I may not refuse

38

your request. If you cannot answer it, you will turn instantly to stone. You understand?

HANS. I understand. (*He moves up* LC)

(*The* QUEEN *moves down* R, *turns and faces Hans*)

QUEEN. Look at me, Hans. Look at the mask of gold which hides my face, and tell me truly what lies beneath. Am I beautiful or am I plain? Which?

(*The* VOICES *are heard*)

LIGHT VOICES (*off*) Beautiful—beautiful—beautiful . . .

DARK VOICES (*off*) Plain—plain—plain . . .

QUEEN. Well, Hans? What is your answer?

(HANS *looks round at the statues as though for advice*)

It's no use appealing to them for help. As you have heard, they cannot even agree among themselves. Well?

HANS (*moving up* C) I'm confused—I don't know—I can't think clearly. (*He moves* LC)

QUEEN. Well?

HANS. You have the air and manner of one who knows she is beautiful, and yet your voice is hard and cruel.

(*The* QUEEN *moves up* C *on to the dais and stands in front of her throne*)

QUEEN. I have given you longer than I gave any of the others. You must answer—now—or be turned to stone. (*She sits on the throne*)

HANS. I cannot believe you are ugly.

QUEEN. What, then, am I?

HANS. Beautiful. You are beautiful.

(*The* QUEEN *rises and moves to Hans*)

QUEEN. I knew what your answer would be the moment you entered my doors. My poor Hans! The incurable romantic who could not believe that a queen could be anything else but beautiful. (*She crosses down* L *of Hans and turns to face him, her back to the audience*) Look at me, Hans. Look at me and see why you have failed.

(HANS *faces the Queen*)

(*She removes her mask*) Do you see? Do you see, now?

HANS. Yes, I see. I was wrong; you should be beautiful, but you are not.

(*The* QUEEN *replaces her mask*)

QUEEN (*with a step towards Han*) You almost make me feel sorry for you, Hans. I could almost let you go—(*she moves nearer to him*) but you now know my secret, and you must not be allowed to reveal it. (*She moves close to him*) You do understand, don't you? (*She pauses*)

Why don't you answer me, Hans? (*She touches his cheek*) How cold you are. As cold as stone—as cold as stone—as cold as stone. (*She turns from him, moves up* C *and sits on her throne*)

The LIGHTS *fade slowly except for a spot on the motionless figure of* HANS. *Presently his voice, softly at first, then louder, comes out of the air calling:* "*Alicia—Alicia. . . .*"

HEIDI

By Beryl M. Jones
From the novel by Johanna Spyri

Heidi, a high-spirited twelve-year-old, has left her uncle's house in the Swiss Alps and has gone to Frankfurt as companion to Klara, a gentle, invalid girl. Heidi is homesick, and Mrs Seseman, Klara's aged grandmother, is kind and sympathetic.

Scene—*A room in the Sesemans' house in Frankfurt.*

Time—1880.

MRS SESEMAN. Come, Heidi, you may look at the pictures.
HEIDI. I have never seen such a lovely big book.

(MRS SESEMAN *turns the pages*)

Oh, what a beautiful one.
MRS SESEMAN. I thought you would like it. It is my favourite too.
HEIDI. Just look at all those animals nibbling at the green grass. The sun is sinking behind the hill, and everything is golden.
MRS SESEMAN. Yes, and here in the midst . . .
HEIDI. Stands the shepherd.
MRS SESEMAN. The Good Shepherd, Heidi.
HEIDI. He is leaning on his crook and watching his flock. I don't think I have ever seen such a lovely scene . . . no, not since . . .
MRS SESEMAN. Since when, Heidi?
HEIDI. Nothing, Grandmamma.
MRS SESEMAN. Tell me, Heidi, why are you suddenly so sad?
HEIDI. Fraulein Rottenheimer says I must be very grateful for staying here and indeed I am. It's . . . it's just that . . .
MRS SESEMAN. Can't you tell me, Heidi?

(HEIDI *shakes her head*)

Very well, my child. Now, how do you think you will like having lessons with the professor? Do you learn easily?
HEIDI. Oh, no.
MRS SESEMAN. No?
HEIDI. I knew before I came to Frankfurt that I would never learn.
MRS SESEMAN. And why not?
HEIDI. Some people can never learn to read. It is far too hard.
MRS SESEMAN. And where did you pick up that wonderful piece of news?

HEIDI. Goat Peter told me. He will never read either.

MRS SESEMAN. Goat Peter, eh? Well, he must be a queer sort of Peter. Now, Heidi, I am going to tell you something. I tell you that, without doubt, you can learn to read, and in a short time too like other children. And now hear what will come next.

HEIDI. When I have learned to read?

MRS SESEMAN. Yes. You saw the Shepherd in the lovely pasture. Now as soon as you have learned to read you shall have that book.

HEIDI. Oh! For my very own?

MRS SESEMAN. For your very own. Then you will be able to read the story about Him.

HEIDI. If only I could read at once!

MRS SESEMAN. That will come very easily if you try.

HEIDI. I will try, very hard. I will listen very carefully and do all the Professor asks me. Will it take longer than a day?

MRS SESEMAN. A day? Why, it will take months. . . .

HEIDI. Months! (*Again her face is clouded and* MRS SESEMAN *gives her a sharp look*)

MRS SESEMAN. Heidi, there is something wrong. I have seen a shadow pass over your face more than once. Can't you tell me what makes that shadow come?

HEIDI. I . . . I have given my word.

MRS SESEMAN. All right, little one. Then I will tell you something more. When one has a sorrow that cannot be told, it must be confided to the Good Shepherd. He will help one bear it. You . . . you pray every day, Heidi?

HEIDI. No, I never do that.

MRS SESEMAN. Have you never learnt to pray, child?

HEIDI. Long ago, but I have forgotten.

MRS SESEMAN. Now I see, little Heidi, why you are unhappy sometimes. It is because you don't know of anyone to help you. Heidi, we must tell the Good Shepherd . . . everything. . . .

HEIDI. Everything?

MRS SESEMAN (*smiling at her and nodding*) Everything, little one.

HEIDI

SCENE—*A room in the Sesemans' house in Frankfurt.*

KLARA. Hullo.

HEIDI. Hello.

KLARA. Do you prefer to be called Heidi or Adelheid?

HEIDI. My name is Heidi and nothing else.

KLARA. Then I will always call you Heidi. Have you always had short curly hair?

HEIDI. Yes, Miss Klara.

KLARA. Call me Klara. Were you glad to come to Frankfurt?

HEIDI. No. Tomorrow I am going back to the Alm.

KLARA. Back? . . . Tomorrow?

HEIDI. Yes, to take Goat Peter's blind grandmother some white rolls.

KLARA. Well, you are a strange one. You have been sent specially to take lessons with me and it turns out you cannot even read. It will all be great fun for me. Now there will be something new at leassons. Just think! Every morning the professor comes . . . at ten o'clock sharp, and the lessons continue until two o'clock. That is so very long. Now that you are here it will be pleasanter and I can listen while you learn to read.

HEIDI. No.

KLARA. Of course, Heidi, you must learn to read. And the professor is so good. He is never, never cross. But listen . . . when he explains something you do not understand . . . and then you still do not understand a single word afterwards, it is best to keep quiet and say nothing or else he will keep on explaining and the more he does the less you will see what he means. Now is there something you would like to ask me?

HEIDI. Yes. Are you very rich?

KLARA. Well, it all depends on what you mean. . . .

HEIDI. Do you—do you think you have as much as five pfennigs.

KLARA. Five pfennigs?

HEIDI. Oh, I do hope that isn't asking too much? You see, I promised the hurdy-gurdy boy that you would give him five pfennigs.

KLARA (*bewildered*) The hurdy-gurdy boy? What hurdy-gurdy boy?

HEIDI. The ragged little boy who plays in the streets. He plays so beautifully and he has a dear little monkey who sits on his shoulder—and he has a tortoise who follows him everywhere on a piece of string.

43

KLARA. But—how did you get to know him?

HEIDI. He was very obliging. You see, I strayed off from my Aunt Dete because I really wanted to find my way back to the Alm. A long way off I could see a tower with a golden ball shining in the sun. I thought if I could climb to the top of the tower I would see where the mountains were . . . and maybe . . . my grandfather's hut and . . .

KLARA. But how does the hurdy-gurdy boy come into all this?

HEIDI. He showed me how to reach the tower. But he said it would cost five pfennigs. I knew you had heaps of money; at least, Aunt Dete said so . . . so . . . so . . . I thought you could easily spare five pfennigs.

KLARA (smiling) Of course I will, Heidi. Do you want the money now?

HEIDI. Oh, no. The boy will call at the house for it. He has gone back to the tower for the kittens.

KLARA. Kittens?

HEIDI. Almost a dozen of them. You see the tower is infested with mice and the keeper has dozens of cats. He was awfully kind to me, and when I didn't even get a glimpse of the Alm when he took me right to the very top of the tower, he promised to let me have some of his kittens instead.

KLARA. How many did you say?

HEIDI. About a dozen . . . they're the loveliest, fluffiest little things . . . I was certain you would love to have them.

KLARA. But, Heidi, Fraulein Rottenheimer hates cats. She almost faints at the sight of one.

HEIDI (crestfallen) Oh!

KLARA. She hates animals of all kinds. . . . But don't look so disappointed. It was very kind of you to think of giving them to me. Come along, perhaps the hurdy-gurdy boy has forgotten to fetch them.

HEIDI. Oh, but . . .

KLARA. Sssh! Here's Fraulein coming back.

JUNIOR MISS

By Jerome Chodorov and Joseph Fields
Based on stories by Sally Benson

Judy and Fuffy are American teenage film fans with a taste for the dramatic. Their vivid imaginations lead them to interfere in other people's lives.

Scene—*The sitting-room of Judy's family.*

Time—*1940.*

Judy (*eyes closed, hears knock*) Come in, Fuffy. . . .

Fuffy (*bouncing in; she is the same age as Judy, not quite so lumpy and prettier*) Oh, doing your Yogi, huh?

Judy. Just a minute. . . . (*Takes a few more deep breaths, as Fuffy sprawls over the sofa watching her*) My mind's much clearer.

Fuffy (*impatiently*) Don't be a goon! Why are you doing your Yogi?

Judy (*rising gravely*) Fuffy, there's a crisis going on in this house.

Fuffy. No kidding? Between who?

Judy. Before I say anything more, I want you to take a sacred vow that this will die with us.

Fuffy (*casually*) Naturally.

Judy. Remember that picture with Joan Crawford and Myrna Loy—*Wife versus Secretary*?

Fuffy (*breathes*) Gosh, yes!

Judy. Well, I think that same kind of thing is developing in this house between my father and Ellen Curtis.

Fuffy (*whistles amazement*) But she's got glasses!

Judy (*impatiently*) So did Myrna Loy . . . when she started out! But after she took them off and got those beauty treatments, she looked gorgeous!

Fuffy (*nods*) Yes, she did! . . . But Ellen's so old! Why she must be . . . she must be . . . twenty-nine!

Judy. Well, after all, Dad's even older than that!

Fuffy. You'd think he'd know better.

Judy. Yes, you would.

Fuffy (*suspiciously*) Judy, are you sure you're not just kicking the gong around?

Judy. It's the truth . . . honestly.

Fuffy. Rat whole?

Judy. Sure.

Fuffy. Well, say it then.

Judy (*holding hand up*) May I swallow a live rat whole if I lie.

45

FUFFY (*nods, convinced*) Well, you better do something, because Myrna Loy certainly made a dope out of that wife!

JUDY. Gee, I'd hate to see Mom in Joan Crawford's position.

FUFFY. I'll speak to your father if you want me to. He may not resent it coming from me.

JUDY. Fuffy! You took a sacred vow!

FUFFY (*firmly*) Well, you'd better do something—and do it quick —before all this tumbles down like a house of cards!

JUDY (*nodding dismally*) Yes, I know it . . . but what can I do?

FUFFY. It's your responsibility! Your father's at that Dangerous Age and he may be starting on his last fling!

JUDY. Oh, Fuffy, do you think so?

FUFFY. But definitely!

(*The telephone rings.* JUDY *answers it*)

JUDY (*elegantly*) Hello! (*Very disappointedly*) Oh, yes, Mrs Adams. . . . Fuffy's here . . . (*Holds the telephone out to* FUFFY *who makes a face as she takes it*)

FUFFY (*surly*) Hello . . . No, what time is it? . . . But, Mother! . . . What tone? I'm not taking any tone. . . . All right, I'll be right down. . . . (*Hangs up grimly*) Heck, a person can't open their mouths! I gotta go to bed!

JUDY (*shakes her head dramatically*) There's no use my even trying to sleep with what's going on in this house.

FUFFY. Yeah. . . . What a mess passion makes out of people's lives.

JUDY. There must be a way out.

FUFFY. There's always a way out with those kind of women. You can always buy them off.

JUDY. Honestly, Fuffy . . . I can't believe Ellen Curtis is that type.

FUFFY (*wisely, eye to eye with Judy*) Just dangle a grand in front of her kisser and you'll see.

JUDY. I'll just have to think of some cheaper way.

FUFFY. Yeah. One of us will get an idea.

JUDY (*nods*) I'll meet you in the lobby after breakfast. . . . Maybe we'll have time for an ice-cream soda before school.

FUFFY. Okay. Well, I'll be seeing you. . . . (*Exits*)

LACE ON HER PETTICOAT

By Aimee Stuart

While Elspeth McNairn is staying with her grandmother, she meets a girl of her own age, the attractive, wealthy Lady Alexandra Carmichael. The two form a friendship, which, because of their social difference, later meets with some disapproval.

SCENE—*The kitchen of a small cottage on the west coast of Scotland.*

PERIOD—*1885.*

ALEXIS (*standing in the doorway*) Hello!

ELSPETH (*turning; surprised*) Hello!

ALEXIS. I stopped the carriage to come and call on you.

ELSPETH. That was rare nice of you. (*She eases* LC) I was wondering how I could get to know you.

ALEXIS (*pleased*) Were you? My name's Alexandra Carmichael—Alexis for short. What's yours?

ELSPETH. Mine's Elspeth.

ALEXIS. May I come in?

ELSPETH. Yes, of course.

ALEXIS (*moving above the table*) You weren't here last year—is your father a new employee on the estate?

ELSPETH. My father's dead.

ALEXIS. Oh, I'm so sorry.

ELSPETH. That's all right—I'm quite used to it by now.

ALEXIS (*easing* R *of the table, then below it*) It's too early for the summer visitors—why are you here?

ELSPETH (*easing to* L *of Alexis*) The doctor ordered me sea-air after I'd had congestion of the lungs.

ALEXIS. What's congestion of the lungs?

ELSPETH. I don't know—but it's awful sore. I had to fight for breath—at one point I was at death's door.

ALEXIS. How interesting. (*She removes her gloves*) What did you think about?

ELSPETH. I don't know—I was unconscious.

ALEXIS. What a pity! I've often wondered what people thought about when they were dying.

ELSPETH. Do you think you should?

ALEXIS. Why not? It's most fearfully interesting. Is your mother here with you?

ELSPETH. No, she's at home in Edinburgh, minding her shop.

ALEXIS. Oh, has she a shop? What kind?

47

ELSPETH. A milliner's. When I leave school I'm to get helping her.

ALEXIS. What fun! Will you be allowed to serve the customers?

ELSPETH. Uh-huh! But not till I've been through the workroom first. Mother believes in learning a thing from A to Z. Is your mother here with you?

ALEXIS (*easing* R) No, she's in Monte Carlo.

ELSPETH. Monte Carlo! Oh, I know about yon. It's a wee principality all on its own, situated between France and Italy. It boasts an Aquarium that's one of the finest in the world. Has your mother maybe gone there to take a look at it?

ALEXIS. Yes, I expect so.

ELSPETH. Why are you not with her?

ALEXIS. Because I've just had measles.

ELSPETH (*crossing to* R *of the table; delighted*) Fancy that! So have I.

ALEXIS. Have you? What fun! Who looked after you?

ELSPETH. My Granny. Who looked after you?

ALEXIS. Oh—Fraulein.

ELSPETH. Who's Fraulein?

ALEXIS. She's my German governess.

ELSPETH (*impressed*) Oh, have you a governess? Do you not go to school, then?

ALEXIS. No, I don't.

ELSPETH. It must be awful lonely learning lessons all by yourself. Would you not rather be with other girls of your own age?

ALEXIS. Yes, I should—much rather.

ELSPETH. Will your parents not let you?

ALEXIS. Not yet—when I'm older, perhaps. Did your mother come to see you when you were ill?

ELSPETH. No. She's the bread-winner—she can't afford to take risks. Did yours come to see you?

ALEXIS. No—she didn't.

ELSPETH. Is she maybe the bread-winner, too, then?

ALEXIS (*amused*) Good gracious, no! You've no idea how funny that sounds.

ELSPETH. Then why did she not come?

ALEXIS. She had too many engagements. I had telegrams and parcels, of course.

ELSPETH (*impressed*) Telegrams! My, how exciting! (*She sits on the chair* R *of the table*) But nothing's the same as seeing your mother, is it?

ALEXIS (*intensely*) No, it is not. (*She pauses*) Do you believe in answer to prayer?

ELSPETH. Of course I do.

ALEXIS. Well, I don't.

ELSPETH (*shocked*) Oh, my, why ever not?

ALEXIS. Did you pray for your mother to come and see you?

ELSPETH. No—I knew she couldn't. I only pray for a thing if there's a fair chance of getting it.

ALEXIS. What's the use of that? They say God can work miracles.

ELSPETH. So He can.

ALEXIS. Then why didn't He let my mother come to see me when I was ill?

ELSPETH. He'll have had a good reason. Maybe there might have been an accident to her train or something.

ALEXIS. Oh, I see. I'll have to think about that. (*She pauses*) I like you—will you be my friend?

ELSPETH. Gladly! I was just requiring a new friend since Granny forbade me to play any more with wee Rosie Colquhoun.

ALEXIS. Rosie Colquhoun?

ELSPETH. Do you know her?

ALEXIS. By sight. My father says the whole wretched family's a disgrace to the estate. He had to dismiss her Uncle Hamish last year for impertinence.

ELSPETH. Oh, my! Is your father maybe the Marquis's overseer, then?

ALEXIS. No—he's the Marquis.

(*There is a pause.* ELSPETH *stares at Alexis*)

ELSPETH. Oh! (*She rises*) Then I don't think I can be your friend.

ALEXIS. Oh, yes, you can—it's quite all right—Fraulein's not with me. She chooses who I can be friends with, but this morning she woke up simply covered with red spots.

ELSPETH. That sounds like the measles.

ALEXIS. I sincerely hope so.

ELSPETH (*shocked*) What a thing to say—don't you like her?

ALEXIS. Like her? Good gracious, no! She makes me drink the skin of hot milk.

ELSPETH (*shuddering*) My, how ghastly! I wouldn't like a person, either, that made me do that.

ALEXIS. I refused it first, no matter how much she punished me. Then at last she thought of a way.

ELSPETH. Oh—what?

ALEXIS (*easing up* C) She stopped me driving with my mother.

ELSPETH. Did your mother let her?

ALEXIS. Yes, of course—one's governess has entire control. She's done wonders with me already—I used to be quite a problem.

ELSPETH. A problem—you—what way?

ALEXIS. I wouldn't do as I was told if I didn't agree with it. (*She glances at the table*) Do you think your grandmother would allow me to stay and have tea with you? (*She eases down* R)

ELSPETH (*delighted*) Aye, I'm sure she would—we have an uncut cake. (*She crosses below the table to the fireplace, lifts the kettle off the hook and stands it on the range*) She's away at the flesher's but she'll be back in a jiffy.

(*The sound of footsteps is heard off*)

There she is.

LISTEN TO THE WIND

By Angela Ainley Jeans

Eleven-year-old Emma has been rescued from the Gypsies by the Gale Bird, and now wakes to find herself on an island.

SCENE—*An island.*

TIME—*Middle of the nineteenth century.*

> (*After a few moments,* EMMA *moves, sits up and rubs her eyes and her head*)

EMMA. Oh, dear! My head hurts. What has happened? I must have been asleep.

> (GALE BIRD *moans and flaps his right wing*)

(*She jumps up and runs to the Gale Bird*) Of course—I remember now—we were falling. Are you all right, or have you been hurt? Why did we fall?

> (GALE BIRD *moans and flaps his left wing*)

Can you talk?

> (GALE BIRD *groans*)

Oh, do try to tell me what is the matter. I cannot help if I do not know your trouble. (*She looks around*)

> (*It is much lighter now*)

We seem to be on an island. (*She pauses. Rather nervously*) A very *little* island. Can you talk, Gale Bird?
GALE BIRD. I think I could, if . . .
EMMA (*after a pause*) If what?
GALE BIRD. If you said a little rhyme. It goes like this:
> "Wind and rain and raging sea,
> Naughty Gale Bird, speak to me."
EMMA (*repeating*)
> "Wind and rain and raging sea,
> Naughty Gale Bird, speak to me."
There now—can you speak?

> (GALE BIRD *faces front and nods*)

Good! But why "Naughty Gale Bird"?
GALE BIRD. I *am* naughty. I let you down.

50

(EMMA *looks up and then down*)

EMMA. Yes, you did, rather. But I do not suppose you could help it. Something must be wrong. What is it?

GALE BIRD. My wing. It hurts dreadfully. (*He moves his right wing a little*)

EMMA. Poor dear. Let me look. (*She looks at the Gale Bird's wing*) Did anything hit it?

(GALE BIRD *shakes his head*)

Well, then, I dare say it is only the cramp. Are you given to cramps?

GALE BIRD. Gale Birds can't have cramp. It isn't done. One feels so silly.

EMMA. I expect you have a little weakness there. Did you ever have a fall?

GALE BIRD. Yes, just now.

EMMA. No, you silly bird. I mean before.

GALE BIRD. I *was* pushed out of my nest when I was a fledgling. East Wind was playing tricks with us.

EMMA. How unkind. (*She feels his wing*)

(*The* GALE BIRD *yelps*)

If only I had some embrocation. Never mind. (*She rubs his wing*) Does that ease the pain?

GALE BIRD. No. Ow!

EMMA. You must be brave. I am afraid it will be worse before it is better. (*She rubs the wing*)

(GALE BIRD *groans*)

(*She stops rubbing*) Do you think we could just pop back and tell Grandmother we are all right?

GALE BIRD. We can't pop anywhere. That's the trouble. I won't be able to fly for ages. I know—I can feel it.

EMMA (*thoughtfully*) We could send a message for another Gale Bird. I mean, sing the song. (*She rubs the wing*)

GALE BIRD (*drawing his wing away*) We could, I suppose. But if you have *any* feeling at all, you'll give me another chance.

EMMA. Why?

GALE BIRD. Gale Birds *can't* have cramp. (*He looks at his wing and tries it*) If we come down when we shouldn't, we are *scorned*. We're not spoken to by anybody. Sometimes even, we are grounded for life.

EMMA. You walk about, you mean?

GALE BIRD. Worse than that. Much worse. (*He pauses*) We can get turned into jellyfish.

EMMA. That is not very pleasant.

(GALE BIRD *affects to weep*)

Then there is nothing for it but to wait here.

GALE BIRD. Very good of you. I'm extremely grateful. (*He preens his wing with his beak*)

(*There is a silence*)

EMMA (*presently*) I am feeling very hungry and rather thirsty. Are you?

GALE BIRD. If I was I could always walk to the sea and drink and catch a fish—that is, if I could walk.

EMMA. But I cannot drink salt water or eat raw fish.

GALE BIRD. You couldn't catch one, anyway. Not with that beak. (*He guffaws*)

EMMA. I find you most ungrateful.

(GALE BIRD *stops laughing*)

I shall take a little walk and see if I can see something to eat or a stream. (*She moves up* L *and picks a bunch of berries*)

(GALE BIRD *hunches up his wing and groans*)

GALE BIRD. What a thing to happen to a Gale Bird. And a Squadron Leader Gale Bird, too. (*He groans*) Poor, poor little me.

EMMA (*crossing to the Gale Bird; excitedly*) Look, look what I've found. Some lovely berries. Rather like blackberries but redder and more juicy. Would you like one?

GALE BIRD. Gale Birds do *not* eat berries. Thanks all the same.

EMMA (*eating greedily*) Most refreshing. I do feel revived.

GALE BIRD. Wish I did. Most painful. Not a *bit* better.

EMMA. I am sorry. I should be rubbing it. (*She crosses to* R *of the Gale Bird and rubs his wing*)

GALE BIRD. Did you say those berries were a bit like blackberries?

EMMA. Yes.

GALE BIRD. But redder?

EMMA. Yes.

GALE BIRD. And more juicy?

EMMA. Yes.

GALE BIRD. And very sweet?

EMMA. Yes. I did.

GALE BIRD. Oh, dear, oh, dear, oh, dear! I am a naughty Gale Bird. I'm a wicked Gale Bird—in fact, I'm silly.

EMMA. Why all that again?

GALE BIRD. Oh, dear, oh, dear, whatever shall we do?

EMMA. Tell me what is the matter.

GALE BIRD. Those berries. They're poison. We heard all about them in Flying School. They're poison—they put you in a trance. They're left about to tempt hungry Gale Birds.

EMMA. Who leaves them about?

GALE BIRD. Sea witches, of course.

EMMA. Who are they?

GALE BIRD. Some mermaids turn into sea witches when they get old. The ones who have never been able to share a sailor.

EMMA. Why should they share sailors?

GALE BIRD (*after a pause*) Someone to talk to, I suppose. Then these old ones lose the use of their tails. They have to swim about on catfish.

(EMMA *moves up* L, *looks around, then returns to* L *of the Gale Bird*)

EMMA (*nervously*) Do you think there are any witches here?

GALE BIRD. Not in daylight, anyway. (*He looks around, then pulls Emma to him and takes her pulse*) Are you sure you're feeling all right?

EMMA. Yes, of course, you silly old bird.

GALE BIRD. Phew! What a relief. I tell you what. You can go on rubbing while I tell you the story of my life.

LITTLE LADYSHIP

By Ian Hay

from the Hungarian of
Stefan Bekeffi & Adorjan Stella

Eve thought that leaving school and being married to famous surgeon, Sir John Brent, would add glamour to her life, but she soon changed her mind, and even envied her schoolgirl cousin, Judy.

Scene—*Sir John's sitting-room.*

Time—*1930.*

Judy. I like your house, dear. H. & C., central heating, modern sanitation. (*She turns*) Hallo, what's the matter? Blubbing?

Eve. No.

Judy. Yes, you are.

Eve. All right—I am. (*She sits L of the settee*)

Judy. Very well, then. I suppose you're not going to tell me why?

Eve. I do so envy you, Judy. When you're going somewhere nothing happens to stop you.

Judy (*sits on the R arm of the settee*) My child, I'd give a good deal if something would happen to stop me going where I've got to go tomorrow.

Eve. Your new school? Who's the Head?

Judy. Name of Philpott. Second in command, Miss Mandrill.

Eve. What are they like?

Judy. There's a technical term for them, I think. "Horrific." "We dare you to see them both in the same programme!"

Eve. Any masters?

Judy. Mr Twemlow, mathematics.

Eve. Old, I suppose?

Judy. Like the last chapter of Mr Chips!

Eve. Have you met any of the girls?

Judy. No, but the dirt's been dished to me by a girl I know. (*Counting on her fingers*) Assorted saps; film fans; baby vamps; teachers' pets and common sneaks. All except Hilda Smithson; she's a pet *and* a sneak.

Eve. Still, she'd be company. What is the food like?

Judy. There's a lot of chat about calories and vitamins, but ! expect it will all boil down to shepherd's pie and stewed prunes.

Eve. I adore them both! Do they work you hard?

JUDY (*slips down into the sofa*) They won't work me hard, but I believe we're all supposed to take the Higher Certificate. But why all this academic curiosity, my child? It's morbid!

EVE (*rises and crosses* R) I wish I'd worked hard and taken the Higher Certificate when I was at St. Anselm's. It might have made me feel more like Jack's intellectual equal. Do you understand?

JUDY. No.

EVE. What games do you play?

JUDY. You take your choice. Polo—tiddley-winks—all-in wrestling . . .

EVE. At St. Anselm's I was captain of lacrosse. Do you play lacrosse?

JUDY. We do. A hellish pastime.

EVE. Have they got a swimming-bath?

JUDY. We have. Average temperature, zero. (*Rises and crosses* L) Let's talk about something else, for Gawd's sake.

EVE (*crosses to Judy*) Judy, one more question. Do they take day girls?

JUDY. Yes, from ten till four—for those who have homes. For me it's a life sentence.

(EVE *crosses to* C, *thinking*)

EVE. Judy, I've got a brainwave.

JUDY. Well?

EVE. I'm afraid to tell you.

JUDY. Don't be so silly.

EVE. You'll laugh.

JUDY. Of course I shall. Come on, tell me.

EVE. It's marvellous—but no, I can't tell you.

JUDY. Oh, come on; of course you can.

EVE (*to* R *of the settee*) All right! I'm going back to school.

JUDY. What? What are you talking about?

EVE. I'm going back to school. I'm going to Tadworthy Lodge as a day-girl.

JUDY. Indeed? Are you bringing your husband with you?

EVE. Jack will never know. I won't have to start in the morning till he's out, and I'll be home long before he gets in.

JUDY. Great Scott, I believe she means it!

EVE. Of course I mean it.

JUDY } (*together*) { You're crazy, raving, crackers and bats . . .
EVE }   { It'll be heaven—girls and games and gossip!

JUDY. But you're past all that. You're a married woman.

EVE. Am I?

JUDY. You're a respectable British matron.

EVE. Who's to know? I wouldn't enter myself as Lady Brent, would I?

JUDY. What are you going to call yourself? Shirley Temple?

EVE. Why not? Something like that, anyhow. (*She jumps on* R *of the settee*) Come on, Judy, help me—it'll be heaps and heaps of fun.

JUDY (*suddenly—climbs on* L *of the settee*) I'm warming up to this, dearie. It'll be a barrel of fun. After all, you can only get spotted and thrown out. It isn't like doing something shady.

EVE. Shady? It's highly educational!

JUDY. Here! (*She takes a form from her case*) Name—age—name of parent or guardian. Guardian—that's the ticket! You'll be a poor orphan and Jack can be the guardian.

EVE. That's an idea!

JUDY. Fill it up. Here's a fountain-pen; let it play. (*She puts the document before Eve and hands her a fountain-pen*)

EVE (*laughing*) What can I call myself? Smith, Jones, Montgomery . . . ?

JUDY. I know. Call yourself—let me see—Ruby Rogers.

EVE. Why?

JUDY. Like dear Ginger, only a different colour. Sign, please.

EVE (*writing*) Ruby Rogers. (*She looks up and laughs*) I've done it! Oh—the address! I can't give this one.

JUDY. Yes, you can. Care of Sir John Brent, Two-fifty Bryanston Square, W.I. You're his ward, my child.

EVE. But—Ruby Rogers? Suppose somebody writes to her—here?

JUDY. Tell Jack she's a girl friend having certain letters addressed here to be forwarded. Slight affair with boy friend. Jack won't mind. Now your age. Sixteen.

EVE. But I look more than that, don't I?

JUDY. No, you don't.

EVE. Sixteen. (*At the foot of the page now*) Signature of parent or guardian authorizing this application! I can't forge Jack's handwriting.

JUDY. I can. Give that to me. (*She takes the form and scribbles on it*) It's one of the things I do really well. There. (*She hands Eve the form*)

EVE (*going over to the mirror* R) But, Judy, I'm sure I don't look sixteen any more. Only a few minutes ago Jack told me I was a woman for the first time.

JUDY. That was your frock, my dear.

EVE. Was it? We'll soon see about that! Let me try yours on.

JUDY. Oke! (*Jumping up*) Come on, off with this nonsense! (*She unfastens the back of Eve's frock*)

(*They begin to take off their dresses, bending down and pulling them right over their heads*)

A LITTLE PRINCESS

By Francess Hodgson-Burnett
adapted from the novel

Sara Crew had to go to Miss Minchin's school, when her father went to sea. Rich, pretty and beautifully dressed, she soon becomes popular especially with little Becky, the kitchen maid. Miss Minchin, a hard, cruel woman is jealous of her attractive pupil's wealth and intelligence.

SCENE—*In Sara's bedroom.*

TIME—*1905.*

SARA (*enters the room and sees Becky asleep by the fire; softly*) Oh! That poor thing! (*Creeps towards her*) I wish she'd waken herself. I don't like to waken her. But Miss Minchin would be cross if she found out. I'll just wait a few minutes . . .

    (*After a pause a piece of coal falls from the fire and* BECKY *wakes with a start*)

BECKY (*jumps up, pulling her cap straight*) Oh, miss! I arst yer pardon, miss! Oh, I do, miss!

SARA (*to her*) Don't be frightened. It doesn't matter the least bit.

BECKY. I didn't go to do it, miss. It was the warm fire—and me bein' so tired, miss. It—it wasn't—imperence.

SARA. You were tired. You could not help it. You are not really awake yet.

BECKY. Ain't—ain't yer angry, miss? Ain't yer goin' ter tell the missus?

SARA. No. Of course I'm not. . . . Why, we are just the same—I am only a little girl like you. It's just an accident that I am not you and you are not me.

BECKY. A' accident, miss . . . is it?

SARA. Yes. . . . Have you done your work? Dare you stay here a few minutes?

BECKY. Here, miss? Me?

SARA (*runs to the door and looks out*) No-one is anywhere about. If your bedrooms are finished, perhaps you might stay a tiny while. I thought perhaps you might like a piece of cake. (*She goes to the cupboard, gets the cake, gives Becky a piece*).

BECKY (*eating hungrily*) Is that—is that there your best? (*Indicates Sara's dress*)

SARA. It is one of my dancing frocks. I like it; don't you?

BECKY (*awed*) Once I see a princess. I was standin' in the street

57

wiv the crowd outside Covin' Garden, watching the swells go inter the operer. An' there was one everyone stared at most. They ses ter each other: "That's the princess." She was a growed-up young lady, but she was pink all over—gowned an' cloak, an' flowers an' all. I called her to mind the minnit I see you, sittin' there on the table, miss. You looked like her.

SARA (*in her reflecting voice*) I've often thought that I should like to be a princess. I wonder what it feels like. I believe I will begin pretending I am one. Becky, were you listening to that story? That I was telling the other girls?

BECKY (*alarmed again*) Yes, miss. I knowed I hadn't orter, but it was that beautiful I—I couldn't help it.

SARA. I liked you to listen to it. If you tell stories you like nothing so much as to tell them to people who want to listen. I don't know why it is. Would you like to hear the rest?

BECKY. Me hear it? Like as if I was a pupil, miss! All about the Prince . . . and the little white mer-babies swimming about laughing . . . with stars in their hair?

SARA. You haven't time to hear it now, I'm afraid, but if you will tell me just what time you come to do my room, I will try to be here and tell you a bit of it every day until it is finished. It's a lovely long one . . . and I'm always putting new bits to it.

BECKY. Then, I wouldn't mind how heavy the coal-boxes was—or what the cook done to me, if—if I might 'ave that ter think of!

SARA. You may. I'll tell it all to you.

(BECKY *exits*.
SARA *sits on the table, feet on a chair, chin in hands*)

SARA. If I was a princess . . . a real princess, I could scatter largess to the populace. But even if I am only a pretend princess I can invent little things to do for people. Things like this. Becky was just as happy as if it was largess. I'll pretend that to do things people like is scattering largess. I've scattered largess.

A LITTLE PRINCESS

SCENE—*In Miss Minchin's sitting-room.*

SARA (*almost to herself*) My papa is dead! My papa is dead! (*To Emily, her doll*) Emily! Do you hear? Do you hear—Papa is dead! He is dead in India—thousands of miles away.

(MISS MINCHIN *enters*)

MISS MINCHIN. Put down your doll! What do you mean by bringing her here?

SARA. No, I will not put her down. She is all I have. My papa gave her to me.

MISS MINCHIN. You will have no time for dolls in future. You will have to work and improve yourself and make yourself useful.

(SARA *stares but does not speak*)

Everything will be very different now. I suppose Miss Amelia has explained matters to you.

SARA. Yes. My papa is dead. He left me no money. I am quite poor.

MISS MINCHIN. You are a beggar. It appears that you have no relations and no home, and no-one to take care of you. What are you staring at? Are you so stupid that you cannot understand? I tell you that you are quite alone in the world, and have no-one to do anything for you, unless I choose to keep you here out of charity.

SARA (*in a low tone*) I understand. I understand.

MISS MINCHIN. That doll . . . that ridiculous doll, with all her nonsensical extravagant things—I actually paid the bill for her.

SARA. The Last Doll . . . the Last Doll. . . .

MISS MINCHIN. The Last Doll, indeed! And she is mine, not yours. Everything you own is mine.

SARA. Please take it away from me then. I do not want it.

MISS MINCHIN. Don't put on grand airs. The time for that sort of thing is past. You are not a princess any longer. Your carriage and your pony will be sent away—your maid will be dismissed. You will wear your oldest and plainest clothes—your extravagant ones are no longer suited to your station. You are like Becky—you must work for your living.

SARA. Can I work? If I can work it will not matter so much. What can I do?

MISS MINCHIN. You can do anything you are told. You are a sharp child and pick up things readily. If you make yourself useful I may

59

let you stay here. You speak French well and you can help with the younger children.

SARA. May I? Oh, please let me! I know I can teach them. I like them, and they like me.

MISS MINCHIN. Don't talk nonsense about people liking you. You will have to do more than teach the little ones. You will run errands and help in the kitchen as well as in the schoolroom. If you don't please me you will be sent away. Remember that. Now go.

(SARA *stands still, looking and thinking. After a pause she turns*)

Stop! Don't you intend to thank me?

SARA (*after a pause*) What for?

MISS MINCHIN. For my kindness to you. For my kindness in giving you a home.

SARA (*turning towards her; fierce, unchild-like*) You are not kind. You are not kind, and it is not a home! (*She runs out of the room*)

THE MAGIC MIRROR

By E. C. BRERETON

Snow-white has fled to the house of the Seven Dwarfs. Her stepmother, the jealous Queen, visits her, disguised as an old woman.

SCENE—*The House of the Seven Dwarfs.*

SNOW-WHITE (*at the table, polishing a glass*) There! (*Holding it up to the light*) I think things look a bit cleaner than they did! Now that's done I think I'll fetch the stockings and get on with the mending before the Seven Dwarfs come home. (*She fetches a large basket of stockings and sits down to mend them*) Hullo! There they are! Nonsense, it's much too early for them to be back. (*She listens*) But I do certainly hear footsteps.

(*A knock at the door*)

Come in! Oh, I forgot! I mustn't open the door. I'll open the window. (*She opens the window*) What do you want, my good woman?

QUEEN (*outside*) It's what do *you* want, my pretty young lady? I've got ribbons and laces, and beads and combs, and pins and needles. All fit for a queen or a pretty little lady like yourself.

SNOW-WHITE. Oh, how sweet! What a lovely necklace! I wish I could see it a little better!

QUEEN. Why don't you come out and look at it, my pretty little lady?

SNOW-WHITE. I can't. The dwarfs say I'm not to go outside the house, for fear my wicked stepmother might send someone to carry me off and kill me.

QUEEN. Why not let me bring my basket inside then, my dear? That would be safe enough, wouldn't it?

SNOW-WHITE. Yes, yes. (*She opens the door*) Come in!

(*Enter the* QUEEN *disguised as an old woman*)

There now. I'll lock the door again. Now no one can creep in to hurt me without my seeing them. Oh! what beautiful things you've got. Let me look at that necklace. Isn't it charming?

QUEEN. Let me fasten it round your pretty white throat, my dear! (*She puts the necklace on Snow-white*) That suits you down to the ground. (*She holds a hand-glass for her*) Doesn't it look nice?

SNOW-WHITE. Yes, it looks beautiful—but it's too tight! It feels as if it would strangle me. The points of the beads prick my neck, and they are so cold and queer. (*She tries to get it off*) I can't undo the clasp. Take it off for me, please.

QUEEN (*aside*) Ah! the poison's beginning to work. (*Aloud*) It'll be all right in a minute. You won't notice it. It only feels tight at first. Just let me comb your hair with this comb, my dear! Isn't that soothing?

SNOW-WHITE. No, it isn't soothing at all. How sharp the teeth are! They're burning my head like fire! Oh, you hurt! I believe the comb is poisoned! You wicked woman! Oh, help me! Help me! I'm dying! (*She falls back*)

QUEEN (*savagely*) Yes, you're quite right. The comb's poisoned, and the necklace is poisoned too, and you are dying. This time you won't come back to mock me as you did before, Snow-white! Last night when I asked my mirror who was the fairest it said:

Snow-white, who lives with the Seven Dwarfs now
 Is fairer, Lady Queen, than thou!

And then I knew the huntsman had *lied* to me, and not killed you, and I tracked you down to do my work myself. And I've done it! You aren't "living" with the Seven Dwarfs now, Snow-white. (*Pause*) But hark! here come the little men!

(*Noise of whistling and dirt being knocked off boots outside*)

I don't want them to find me here. I must fly.

MAKE BELIEVE

By A. A. Milne

Anxious to find a husband for his daughter, the King sets a test for three Princes, but the Princess has already decided to marry the woodcutter.

Scene—*In the wood.*

> The Woodcutter *is discovered singing at his work, in a glade of the forest outside his hut. He is tall and strong, and brave and handsome; all that a woodcutter ought to be. Now it happened that the* Princess *was passing, and as soon as his song is finished, sure enough, on she comes.*

Princess. Good morning, Woodcutter.

Woodcutter. Good morning. (*But he goes on with his work*)

Princess (*after a pause*) Good morning, Woodcutter.

Woodcutter. Good morning.

Princess. Don't you ever say anything except good morning?

Woodcutter. Sometimes I say good-bye.

Princess. You *are* a cross woodcutter today.

Woodcutter. I have work to do.

Princess. You are still cutting wood? Don't you ever do anything else?

Woodcutter. Well, you are still a Princess; don't *you* ever do anything else?

Princess (*reproachfully*) Now, that's not fair, Woodcutter. You can't say I was a Princess yesterday, when I came and helped you stack your wood. Or the day before, when I tied up your hand where you had cut it. Or the day before that, when we had our meal together on the grass. Was I a Princess then?

Woodcutter. Somehow I think you were. Somehow I think you were saying to yourself, "Isn't it sweet of a Princess to treat a mere woodcutter like this?"

Princess. I think you're perfectly horrid. I've a good mind never to speak to you again. (*Turns* R) And—and I would, if only I could be sure that you would notice I wasn't speaking to you.

Woodcutter. After all, I'm just as bad as you. Only yesterday I was thinking to myself how unselfish I was to interrupt my work in order to talk to a mere Princess.

Princess. Yes, but the trouble is that you *don't* interrupt your work.

Woodcutter (*interrupting it and going up to her with a smile*) Madam, I am at your service.

Princess. I wish I thought you were.

63

WOODCUTTER. Surely you have enough people at your service already. Princes and Chancellors and Chamberlains and Waiting Maids.

PRINCESS. Yes, that's just it. That's why I want your help. Particularly in the matter of Princes.

WOODCUTTER. Why, has a suitor come for the hand of her Royal Highness?

PRINCESS. Three suitors. And I hate them all.

WOODCUTTER. And which are you going to marry?

PRINCESS. I don't know. Father hasn't made up his mind yet.

WOODCUTTER. And this is a matter which father—which His Majesty decides for himself?

PRINCESS. Why, of course! You should read the history books, Woodcutter. The suitors to the hand of a Princess are always set some trial of strength or test of quality by the King and the winner marries his daughter.

WOODCUTTER. Well, I don't live in a Palace, and I think my own thoughts about these things. I'd better get back to work. (*He goes on with his chopping*)

PRINCESS (*gently, after a pause*) Woodcutter!

WOODCUTTER (*looking up*) Oh, are you there? I thought you were married by this time.

PRINCESS (*meekly*) I don't want to be married. (*Hastily*) I mean, not to any of those three.

WOODCUTTER. You can't help yourself.

PRINCESS. I know. That's why I wanted *you* to help me.

WOODCUTTER (*going up to her*) Can a simple woodcutter help a Princess?

PRINCESS. Well, perhaps a simple one couldn't, but a clever one might.

WOODCUTTER. What would his reward be?

PRINCESS. His reward would be that the Princess, not being married to any of her three suitors, would still be able to help him chop his wood in the mornings. . . . I *am* helping you, aren't I?

WOODCUTTER (*smiling*) Oh, decidedly.

PRINCESS (*nodding*) I thought I was.

WOODCUTTER. It is kind of a great lady like yourself to help so humble a fellow as I.

PRINCESS (*meekly*) I'm not *very* great. (*And she isn't. She is the smallest, daintiest little Princess that ever you saw*)

WOODCUTTER. There's enough of you to make a hundred men unhappy.

PRINCESS. And one man happy?

WOODCUTTER. And one man very, very happy.

PRINCESS (*innocently*) I wonder who he'll be. . . . Woodcutter, if *you* were a Prince, would you be my suitor?

WOODCUTTER (*scornfully*) One of three?

PRINCESS (*excitedly*) Oo, would you kill the others? With that axe?

WOODCUTTER. I would not kill them, in order to help His Majesty make up his mind about his son-in-law. But if the Princess had made up her mind—and wanted me . . .

PRINCESS. Yes?

WOODCUTTER. Then I would marry her, however many suitors she had.

PRINCESS. Well, shes' only got three at present.

WOODCUTTER. What is that to me?

PRINCESS. Oh, I just thought you might want to be doing something to your axe.

WOODCUTTER. My axe?

PRINCESS. Yes. You see, she *has* made up her mind.

WOODCUTTER (*amazed*) You mean . . . But—but I'm only a wood-cutter.

PRINCESS. That's where you'll have the advantage of them when it comes to axes.

WOODCUTTER. Princess! (*He takes her in his arms*) My Princess!

PRINCESS. Woodcutter! My Woodcutter! My, oh so very slow and uncomprehending, but entirely adorable woodcutter!

WOODCUTTER. But what will His Majesty say?

PRINCESS. All sorts of things. . . . Do you really love me, Wood-cutter, or have I proposed to you under a misapprehension?

WOODCUTTER. I adore you!

PRINCESS (*nodding*) I thought you did. But I wanted to hear you say it. If I had been a simple peasant, I suppose you would have said it a long time ago?

WOODCUTTER. I expect so.

PRINCESS (*nodding*) Yes. . . . Well, now we must think of a plan for making Mother like you.

WOODCUTTER. Might I just kiss you again before we begin?

PRINCESS. Well, I don't quite see how I am to stop you.

(*The* WOODCUTTER *picks her up in his arms and kisses her*)

WOODCUTTER. There!

PRINCESS (*in his arms*) Oh, Woodcutter, Woodcutter, why didn't you do that the first day I saw you? Then I needn't have had the bother of proposing to you. (*He puts her down suddenly*) What is it?

WOODCUTTER (*listening*) Somebody coming. (*He peers through the trees and then says in surprise*) The King!

PRINCESS. Oh! I must fly!

WOODCUTTER. But you'll come back?

PRINCESS. Perhaps.

THE MEMBER OF THE WEDDING

By CARSON McCULLERS

*Frankie Addams is a lonely, gangly, overgrown twelve-year-old, motherless
and with few friends and a feeling of belonging nowhere. John Henry is
seven years old, a self-contained, lovable boy.*

SCENE—*The Addams's living-room.*

TIME—*1946.*

> *Frankie has been left alone in the house. She is lonely and decides to call
> her cousin, John Henry, in to spend the night with her.*

FRANKIE. Seems like everybody goes off and leaves me. (*Calls*)
John Henry! John Henry!

JOHN HENRY (*off*) What do you want, Frankie?

FRANKIE. Come over and spend the night with me.

JOHN HENRY (*off*) I can't.

FRANKIE. Why?

JOHN HENRY (*off*) Just because.

FRANKIE. Because why? (*John Henry does not answer*) I thought
maybe me and you could put up my Indian tepee and sleep out
here in the yard. And have a good time. (*There is still no answer*) Sure
enough. Why don't you stay and spend the night?

JOHN HENRY (*off; quite loudly*) Because, Frankie, I don't want to.

FRANKIE (*angrily*) Fool Jackass! Suit yourself! I only asked you
because you looked so ugly and lonesome.

JOHN HENRY (*coming in*) Why, I'm not a bit lonesome.

FRANKIE. I wonder when that Papa of mine is coming home. He
always comes home by dark. I don't want to go into that empty
ugly house all by myself.

JOHN HENRY. Me neither.

FRANKIE (*standing with outstretched arms and looking around her*) I
think something is wrong. It is too quiet. I have a peculiar warning
in my bones. I bet you a hundred dollars it's going to storm.

JOHN HENRY. I don't want to spend the night with you.

FRANKIE. A terrible, terrible dog-day storm. Or maybe even a
cyclone.

JOHN HENRY. Huh.

FRANKIE. I bet Jarvis and Janice are now at Winter Hill. I see
them just as plain as I see you. Plainer. Something is wrong. It's too
quiet.

(*A clear horn begins to play a blues tune in the distance*)

66

JOHN HENRY. Frankie?
FRANKIE. Hush! It sounds like Honey.

(*The horn music becomes jazzy and spangling, then the first blues tune is repeated. Suddenly while still unfinished the music stops.* FRANKIE *waits tensely*)

FRANKIE. He has stopped to bang the spit out of his horn. In a second he will finish. (*After a wait*) Please, Honey, go on, finish.
JOHN HENRY (*softly*) He done quit now.
FRANKIE (*moving restlessly*) I told Berenice that I was leaving town for good and she did not believe me. Sometimes I honestly think that she is the biggest fool that ever drew breath. You try to impress something on a big fool like that, and it's just like talking to a block of cement. I kept on telling and telling and telling her. I told her I had to leave this town for good because it is inevitable. Inevitable.
JOHN HENRY. You want me to get the week-end bag?
FRANKIE. Don't bother me, John Henry, I'm thinking.
JOHN HENRY. What you thinking about?
FRANKIE. About the wedding. About my brother and the bride. Everything's been so sudden today. I never believed before about the fact that the earth turns at the rate of about a thousand miles a day. I didn't understand why it was that if you jumped up in the air you wouldn't land in Selma or Fairview or somewhere else instead of the same back-yard. But now it seems to me I feel the world going around very fast. (*She begins turning around in circles with arms outstretched*)

(JOHN HENRY *copies her. They both turn*)

I feel it turning and it makes me dizzy.
JOHN HENRY. I'll stay and spend the night with you.
FRANKIE (*suddenly stopping her turning*) No. I just now thought of something.
JOHN HENRY. You just a little while ago was begging me.
FRANKIE. I know where I'm going.

(*There are sounds of children playing in the distance*)

JOHN HENRY. Let's go play with the children, Frankie.
FRANKIE. I tell you I know where I'm going. It's like I've known it all my life. Tomorrow I will tell everybody.
JOHN HENRY. Where?
FRANKIE (*dreamily*) After the wedding I'm going with them to Winter Hill. I'm going off with them after the wedding.
JOHN HENRY. You serious?
FRANKIE. Shush, just now I realized something. The trouble with me is that for a long time I have been just an "I" person. All other people can say "we". When Berenice says "We" she means her lodge and church and coloured people. Soldiers can say "We" and mean the army. All people belong to a "we" except me.

JOHN HENRY. What are we going to do?

FRANKIE. Not to belong to a "we" makes you too lonesome. Until this afternoon I didn't have a "we", but now after seeing Janice and Jarvis I suddenly realize something.

JOHN HENRY. What?

FRANKIE. I know that the bride and my brother are the "we" of me. So I'm going with them and joining with the wedding. This coming Sunday when my brother and the bride leave this town, I'm going with the two of them to Winter Hill. And after that to whatever place that they will ever go. (*There is a pause*) I love the two of them so much and we belong to be together. I love the two of them so much because they are the "we" of me.

NATIONAL VELVET

By Enid Bagnold

A strange affinity exists between Mrs Brown, an ex-Channel swimmer, and her daughter, Velvet, who has just won a piebald horse. Mi is her father's odd-job man; his father trained Mrs Brown to swim the Channel and he thinks Velvet could be trained to win the Grand National.

Scene—*Outside the Browns' cottage in Sussex.*

Time—*The 1930's.*

VELVET *rushes to her mother.*

VELVET. Mother! . . . I gotta tell you. . . . I'll tell you now! . . . Mi's in the street . . . waiting . . . he's just gone. . . . It's him an' me. Mi an' me together!

(*A shudder goes through* MRS. BROWN. *She does not move, or respond when* VELVET *catches her sleeve*)

Mi an' me . . . Mother, sit down! Sit down, won't you! . . . I can't tell you while you stand like that, Mother, looking at me. . . . (*She pauses, stares at her mother, who slowly sits, fearing what Velvet is going to tell her.* VELVET *kneels by her, one hand on her mother's knee, Mrs Brown does not take it*) We think . . . we think The Piebald . . . .

MRS BROWN. What's that?

VELVET (*faintly*) We think . . . he's fit . . . to run . . . run fit to in the . . . National. . . . (*She sits back breathless*)

(MRS BROWN *is filled with relief, she relaxes*)

MRˢ BROWN. Almighty God!

(VELVET *stands, stares at her mother.* MRS BROWN *finds any news unimportant to what she had expected. She speaks mechanically*)

What's that you're telling me? Velvet? In the National?

VELVET (*whispering*) Thought . . . of running him. . . .

MRS BROWN. Mi Taylor an' his miracles! That's what they are! The two of 'em the same. Mi—an' his miracles!

VELVET (*not understanding*) Mother!

MRS BROWN. Father and son. There's no end to what they think people can do! The Grand National with them jumps?

VELVET. Thirty jumps. Fifteen jumps twice round. . . .

MRS BROWN (*with a slight laugh*) Stiff. Yes. An' stiff. Where's Mi? With you telling me this?

69

VELVET. He's outside. Waiting.

MRS BROWN. He better be. You fetch him in. Cut along now to your bed. That's enough for one night.

VELVET (*low*) There's more, Mother.

MRS BROWN. There is?

VELVET. I couldn't do it if I didn't tell you. I gotta tell you all. You gotta pretend I'm not your child.

MRS BROWN (*steadily*) What's that, Velvet?

VELVET (*gulping*) You was nineteen when you swum the Channel. I'm fourteen, but my chance's come early. You mustn't think I'm your child. (*Looking up suddenly and speaking strongly*) I'm a girl with a Chance!

(MRS BROWN *stands*. VELVET *goes to her and looks in her face*)

Nobody kin ride him like I can, Mother. He knows me, he knows every thought I think.

MRS BROWN (*taking Velvet's shoulder*) What's that? In the race, Velvet? Is that what you're telling me? Is that what you've got in your head? Is Mi in on this?

VELVET. Mi an' me . . . we . . . think . . . I kin ride that horse.

MRS BROWN. Are you daft?

VELVET. Was you daft?

MRS BROWN. I was nineteen.

VELVET. You got to take your chance when it comes. Mi an' me, we've thought it all out. If you ask him he can tell you every step how it can come true. If I'm found out the worst they can do is to send me home . . . an' father 'll be angry. Just as likely I won't be found out. Well, then, we'll do our best. The horse is great. You know he is. He's like a Bible horse.

(MRS BROWN *leaves Velvet and goes to the dresser, supporting herself against it*)

MRS BROWN. I'll listen to you, Velvet. I'll listen to you in a minute. You stop where you are an' let me get me breath. (*She turns, facing front, still leaning on the dresser*) But I don't want to speak to Mi about it. Tell him not to speak to me about it. Not a word. (*She pants a little*) If I'm to give my leave let there be no whisperin' an' talking. I can't be but your mother, Velvet. It's goin' to be a weight upon me. I mus' take it in. I mus' understand it. Then . . . I must put it from me, an' pray to God. . . .

NO ROOM AT THE INN

By Joan Temple

Norma, a precocious, but warm-hearted cockney, and Mary, a well-brought-up, now motherless girl, are two of five evacuees billeted with the slatternly Mrs Voray.

SCENE—*The living-room of Mrs. Voray's house.*

TIME—*During the Second World War.*

> *Norma is standing with her hands behind her back, trying to recite the poem she has to memorize for homework, though her thoughts are really engaged by what is happening outside the window. Mary is sitting prompting her from the book in her hand.*

NORMA. "Bring me my bow of burning gold . . ." (*Straining her neck to look out*) Eer-rum—gold. (*Clicks her tongue*)

MARY (*coarsely*) Oh, get on with it!

NORMA. Well, it's so soppy! That's why I can't get it into me head. Why can't Mrs Drave give us something with a story in it. (*Giggling*) Ireen's got a nice piece to learn, she says. It's called: "How they brought the good news to the Gents".

MARY. Yer silly fathead! It's "How they brought the good news to Ghent"!

NORMA. Oh? (*Sniffs*) Not *my* style, dearie!

MARY. D'yer want me to hear yer piece, or don't yer?

> (NORMA *takes two sweets wrapped in paper from a secret pocket under her skirt and hands one to* MARY)

Ooh! Thanks a lot!

> (NORMA *starts to unwrap the sweet*)

'Ere! Yer can't say yer piece with a sucker in yer mouth. Yer jaws'll get stuck. And I want to get out and find Ronnie.

NORMA (*holding the sweet in the paper with one end unwrapped*) All right, then, I'll just have a suck now and then to keep up me strength. Where was I? Ah! (*Gabbling*) "Bring me my bow of burning gold bring me my arrers of desire bring me my spur—Ho!" Ho what?

MARY. "Oh, clouds unfold . . ."

NORMA. Ain't it tripe?

MARY. It isn't! It's lovely! Why, it's—it's a classic!

NORMA. What's a classic?

MARY. It's—oh, *you* know what a classic is.

NORMA. No, I don't. And you don't, neither.

MARY. Yes, I do, then. A classic—well, a classic is something by a dead Englishman or a live foreigner.

NORMA. Sounds punk to *me!*

MARY. Oh, get on!

NORMA. Where was I?

MARY. "Oh, clouds unfold . . ."

NORMA (*after a lick*) "Ho, clouds unfold 'n bring me . . ." Er—what do I want 'em to bring me now?

MARY (*sucking sweet*) "Chariot of fire."

NORMA. "Chariot of fire." Er—rum—ooh, old Charlie Pearson's just going along! (*Diving under curtain*) Wotcher, Chawlie! I'll be seeing yer!

MARY (*insistently*) "I will not cease . . ."

NORMA (*coming out from under the curtain*) What?

MARY. "I will not cease . . ."

NORMA. Yers. But what won't I cease *from?*

MARY. "Mental strife, nor . . ."

NORMA. "Nor shall my sword . . ."

MARY. *Sword!*

NORMA. "Sword sleep in my 'and—*Hand*," (*Gabbling*) "Till we have built Jeruslem in h'England's green and pleasant land." What does *that* mean? Have the Jews all over England?

MARY (*taking out her sweet and wrapping it in the paper*) I think it means everybody being happy.

NORMA. What, free pictures and pally-de-dances? (*Sketching an arabesque*) Whoopee!

MARY. No. I think it means something spiritual.

NORMA (*darkly*) Ha! That's where they have you!

MARY (*cynically*) Not half, they don't! (*Hurling the book at Norma*) Oh, take the bleeding book away! I *hate* that poem!

NORMA (*glancing out of the window*) Here's old Ma Waters coming in! You can guess what *she's* coming for—bed and breakfast and no questions!

MARY (*rising*) I'm going out to find old Ron.

NORMA. Why don't yer come along with me and the boys? Don't want to be everlasting playing with a soppy kid like Ronnie. You *are* soft!

MARY. I'm not, then! You call me soft again and I'll slap yer silly face. And I won't have yer making fun of Ronnie, see?

NORMA. Him? Slopping cry-baby!

MARY (*vehemently*) Well, you let him alone or I—I'll tear your eyes out! Get me?

NORMA (*impressed*) And I believe yer would, too. (*Sketching another arabesque*) Wish Mum 'ud get me a job as a child dancer. Might get on the films and make a fortune. (*Makes an extraordinary face*) *I* could do that innocent baby stuff, all right, all right. Don't you think I look rather like Shirley Temple? (*She raises her eyes to the sky*)

MARY. Yes, if Shirley Temple could ever look so lousy!
NORMA (*furious*) You little cat! I'll . . .

MARY *makes a dash for the door, slamming it behind her in Norma's face.*

PINK STRING AND SEALING WAX

By ROLAND PERTWEE

Myra Strachan is mending socks, while Eva, her twelve-year-old daughter reluctantly stitches a sampler. She is the youngest of four—an ugly duckling with an insatiable curiosity. The father is a chemist in Brighton.

SCENE—*The parlour of the Strachan's house.*

TIME—*1880.*

EVA. Mama.

MRS STRACHAN. Yes, dear?

EVA. Lucy caught a mouse this morning.

MRS STRACHAN. Poor thing!

EVA. But she didn't drown it. Pa said to give any mice she caught to him.

MRS STRACHAN (*changing the subject*) I cannot imagine how Father makes such enormous potatoes in his socks.

EVA. Why would Pa want mice?

MRS STRACHAN. I don't know, dear. To put them out of their misery, perhaps.

EVA (*ponders this*) Oh. Is that why we say, "Pity mice implicitly"?

MRS STRACHAN. We say nothing of the kind.

EVA. I do. Every night in my prayers. Gentle Jesus, meek and mild, look on me a little child . . . pity mice implicitly.

MRS STRACHAN. No, no, Eva. Pity my *simplicity*.

EVA. Oh. Perhaps the other would do more good. Mice have a much horrider time than my simplicity does.

MRS STRACHAN. Where's Jessie?

EVA. Doing Ophelia in front of the looking-glass, Mama.

MRS STRACHAN. Doing Ophelia?

EVA. Acting, Mama.

MRS STRACHAN. I do wish she wouldn't. Father would never approve of one of his daughters going on the stage.

EVA. Why not?

MRS STRACHAN. Get on with your work.

EVA. Why were samplers ever invented?

MRS STRACHAN. To teach young people difficult stitches which will be useful when they grow up.

EVA (*looking at the sampler with hostility*) How would Eva Strachan, aged twelve. . . . ABCDEFG . . . 1234567 be useful to somebody who means to be a dancer?

MRS STRACHAN. It would teach her to be industrious and patient.

Eva. I don't think Pa can ever have made a sampler. He isn't a bit patient.

Mrs Strachan. How many times have I told you not to criticize your elders and betters?

Eva (*after a pause*) What's Pa better than?

Mrs Strachan. Better than?

Eva. If he's better he must be better than something. Is he better than something? Is he better than any other chemist in Brighton?

Mrs Strachan. Much better.

Eva. Are you proud of Pa being a chemist?

Mrs Strachan (*shortly*) Yes.

Eva. When anybody asks me what he is, I say he's the Public Analyst.

Mrs Strachan. A, dear, not The.

Eva. Public Analysts do murders, don't they?

Mrs Strachan. Eva!

Eva. I don't mean themselves, but to bits of people who've been murdered. They boil up their tummies to find out who did it.

Mrs Strachan. Eva!

Eva. I 'spect Pa's boiling one up now.

Mrs Strachan. Your father is analysing a sample of milk from that new dairy.

Eva. Doctors and policemen bring them in jars and bottles. Little Lily heard a tummy wergling in its jar, and one night Malcolm rushed into my room and said a ghost was howling round the house because it felt empty inside.

Mrs Strachan (*terribly upset*) Oh, dear! Father was most anxious the children should know nothing of that side of his work. Who told you, Eva? Eva, who told you?

Eva (*hedging*) I've done my "N" upside down.

Mrs Strachan. I'm certain it wasn't Emily. She's much too sensible. . . . Nellie Martin! Tch, tch!

Eva. The one whose sister married a public-house?

Mrs Strachan. Publican, my dear, not house. I knew that girl had a bad influence and wasn't steady.

Eva. Can you tell a person isn't steady by searching their box?

Mrs Strachan. If you find something that shouldn't be there, you certainly can.

Eva. Jessie says you sent her away because her sister Pearl shrieked with laughter in the kitchen and made her eyes big at Albert.

Mrs Strachan. Eva, be quiet!

Eva. I wish I'd seen her, but I was always in bed when she came.

Mrs Strachan. A good thing too.

Eva. I never have seen a person make their eyes big at anybody. Why do they?

Mrs Strachan. That will do!

PINOCCHIO

By BRIAN WAY and WARREN JENKINS

Gepetto, an old puppet-maker, wishes for a log to make a puppet. The wood-seller gives him the wood, and Gepetto sets to work on it. As Pinocchio is chiselled out of the log, the Fairy breathes life into it.

SCENE—*Gepetto's house.*

GEPETTO *sets eagerly to work. He hits once with the chisel and there is a flash and a puff of smoke. He dashes to the front of the stage area to the audience.*

GEPETTO. Good Heavens! Did I do that? (*He turns and we see the completed puppet lying motionless on its back. He moves toward it, looks at it from all sides, and then comes back to the audience*)

GEPETTO. That was quick, wasn't it? My chisel hardly touched it. (*He returns and looks again at the puppet, mumbling about how nice it is. Then suddenly, he has a thought and returns to the audience*)

GEPETTO. Oh, dear—I've forgotten something. I haven't thought of a name for him. Oh, dear, how difficult it is. Now what should I call him, d'you think? What was that? Pinocchio? Pinocchio! Well, that sounds nice—I think. Pinocchio! Pinocchio! Yes, yes. I like that. Wonder what he'll think of it.

PINOCCHIO. It's all right.

(GEPETTO *freezes—with his back to Pinocchio*)

GEPETTO. Did you—did you—hear—that? It—it—he—spoke. Didn't he? My puppet. He spoke. Oh, how wonderful. It's come true. My wish—it's come true. Or did I imagine it? I'll try again. (*He tiptoes to Pinocchio—is about to speak—then can't bring himself to, so tiptoes back to the audience*) Oh, dear, I don't like to try again. I mean just suppose I *had* only imagined it? Hmmmm? Still, I must find out sometime. Oh! I know. (*He screws his face up and puts his hands over it*)

GEPETTO (*in half-whisper*) Pin—Pinocchio! Pinocchiooo!

PINOCCHIO. Hello. Where are you?

GEPETTO. It is. It is true. (*He runs to Pinocchio*) Here I am, Pinocchio. Here I am.

PINOCCHIO. What's Pinocchio?

GEPETTO. Your name.

PINOCCHIO. Oh. What's yours?

GEPETTO. Gepetto.

PINOCCHIO. Gepetto! Oh, well why can't I be called Gepetto, too?

GEPETTO. Well, that would be a bit confusing, wouldn't it?

PINOCCHIO. Yes, I suppose it would. Well, aren't you going to help me up? I'm getting a bit stiff lying here.

GEPETTO. Oh, I'm sorry. I was so excited, I forgot. Of course I'll help you up. Now up you come—urrrp—there—right—up—on—your—feet. (*He gets Pinocchio right up on his feet—then he takes his arms away and Pinocchio drops in a heap. Gepetto runs to his aid*)

GEPETTO. Oh, dear, oh, dear, oh, dear. Oh, don't tell me you've got to have strings like all the others. Oh, I had so hoped . . .

PINOCCHIO. Strings. What strings?

GEPETTO. Well, you see, most puppets work by strings—but I hoped you'd be able to manage without.

PINOCCHIO. And I shall. Come on, give me a hand. It's only a matter of practice—isn't it?

GEPETTO. Yes. I suppose it is.

THE PRINCESS AND THE GOBLIN

By GEORGE MacDONALD
adapted from the novel

Irene, a pretty eight-year-old Princess, bored with the numerous toys in her nursery, begins to explore an old steep staircase, and in a room at the top finds an old lady spinning. The old lady has long white hair, but is tall and straight, with no stoop; her face is smooth, but her eyes are very wise.

SCENE—*A room at the top of a staircase.*

> IRENE *has been crying and* GRANDMOTHER *has washed her face.*

GRAN. There, That looks a bit better and fresher.

IRENE. Oh, thank you so much for washing my face. You have such soft hands.

GRAN (*smiling*) Do you know my name, child?

IRENE. No, I don't know it.

GRAN. My name is Irene.

IRENE. That's *my* name.

GRAN. I know that. I let you have mine. I haven't got your name. You've got mine.

IRENE. How can that be. I've always had my name.

GRAN. Your papa, the King, asked me if I had any objection to your having it, and of course I hadn't. I let you have it with pleasure.

IRENE. It was very kind of you to give me your name—and such a pretty one.

GRAN. Oh, not so very kind! A name is one of those things one can give away and still keep all the same. I have a good many such things. Wouldn't you like to know who I am, child?

IRENE. Yes, that I should—very much.

GRAN. I'm your great-great-grandmother.

IRENE. What's that?

GRAN. I'm your father's mother's father's mother.

IRENE. Oh, dear! I can't understand that!

GRAN. I dare say not. I didn't expect you would. But that's no reason why I shouldn't say it.

IRENE. Oh, no.

GRAN. I will explain it all to you when you are older. But you will be able to understand this much now: I came here to take care of you.

IRENE. Is it long since you came? Was it yesterday? Or was it to-day because it was so wet that I couldn't get out.

GRAN. I've been here ever since you came yourself.

IRENE. What a long time. I don't remember it at all.

GRAN. No, I suppose not.

IRENE. But I never saw you before.

GRAN. No, but you shall see me again.

IRENE. Do you live in this room always?

GRAN. I don't sleep in it. I sleep on the opposite side of the landing. I sit here most of the day.

IRENE. I shouldn't like it. My nursery is much prettier. You must be a Queen too, if you are my great big grandmother.

GRAN. Yes, I am a Queen.

IRENE. Where is your crown then?

GRAN. In my bedroom.

IRENE. I *should* like to see it.

GRAN. You shall some day—not today.

IRENE. I wonder why Nursie never told me.

GRAN. Nursie doesn't know. She never saw me.

IRENE. But somebody knows that you are in the house?

GRAN. No, nobody.

IRENE. How do you get your dinner then?

GRAN. I keep poultry—of a sort.

IRENE. Where do you keep them?

GRAN. I will show you.

IRENE. And who makes the chicken broth for you?

GRAN. I never kill any of my chickens.

IRENE. That I can't understand.

GRAN. What did you have for breakfast this morning?

IRENE. Oh, I had bread and milk and an egg—I dare say you eat their eggs.

GRAN. Yes, that's it. I eat their eggs.

IRENE. Is that what makes your hair so white?

GRAN. No, my dear, I'm very old. It's old age.

IRENE. I thought so. Are you fifty?

GRAN. Yes, more than that.

IRENE. Are you a hundred?

GRAN. Yes—more than that. I am too old for you to guess. Come and see my chickens. Would you like to?

IRENE. Oooh! Yes, please.

They go out

THE PRINCESS AND THE PLAYERS

By Barbara Watts

Elizabeth, later Queen of England, is staying with her friend, Anne, in the house of Anne's aunt, the Lady Eleanor, Countess of Marshlake. Elizabeth is eight, red-haired and fiery tempered. Anne, a dark, demure ten-year-old, is sewing in the garden when Elizabeth rushes in.

SCENE—*The garden of Lady Eleanor's home, near London.*

TIME—*1541.*

ELIZABETH. Fourteen times! And I still don't feel a bit better. And I haven't seen anything . . . what was I supposed to see?

ANNE. Nothing, silly. I didn't say you were supposed to see anything in particular. I only said that if you were tired of sitting still, you might try walking fourteen times round the rose garden to see what you could see.

ELIZABETH. Well, there's nothing to see, thank you. Just a waste of time.

ANNE (*placidly*) There's no point in your saving time anyway, you don't know what to do with it when you've got it, even though you *are* Princess Elizabeth.

ELIZABETH. Oh, dear, we're going to quarrel, I know we are, and I don't want to a bit, but if you sit there with that stupid bit of sewing much longer, I shall give you a good hard smack. . . . I can feel it coming. . . . Oh, Anne, do come and play something.

ANNE. But Aunt Eleanor said we were to stay quietly here until she came back with her book.

ELIZABETH (*coming down to the bench and trying to take away Anne's sewing*) Well, I'm not asking you to climb trees, or stand on your head in the fountain. I only want you to play, instead of sticking that needle in and pulling it out again.

ANNE. I don't like your games. They're silly.

ELIZABETH. This one won't be, really, Anne. Let's pretend we're soldiers, marching to battle. . . . No, no. . . . I'll be a Queen and you be a courtier coming to dance with me. I'll say . . . oh, come on, Anne. (*She pulls her to her feet*) Let's practise that last dance Master Ferrars taught us.

(*They dance a few steps*—ELIZABETH *eagerly and with more enjoyment than skill and* ANNE *soberly, with dainty, correct steps. Suddenly* ELIZABETH *seizes Anne's two hands, and swings her gaily round and round,* ANNE *breaks away, indignant*)

ANNE. There you go. You're always the same . . . either you're rough or you play silly games, all about fairies and moonbeams.

ELIZABETH (*throwing herself repentantly on the ground beside Anne*) Oh, dear, I'm so sorry. But it is so dull here. I'd rather be in London, than in this poky garden. Nothing ever happens.

ANNE. But I thought you said a little while ago that you were tired of London, that it was stuffy, and you seemed glad when Aunt Eleanor invited you to come and stay with her. I think it's very nice here, with these lovely flowers, and horses to ride. And, anyway, Aunt Eleanor isn't your aunt, you know.

ELIZABETH. I know, and I didn't mean to be rude. I think it's nice of Lady Eleanor to have me. But I do want exciting things to happen to me, and wherever I am they never do. I can't understand it.

ANNE. But what do you want to happen?

ELIZABETH. I don't know. . . . I want to see lots of people, to have a gay time, and dance, and have songs written about me, and have soldiers to go to war for me. I should like lots of frocks, and heaps of nice things to eat. I want to go to France, and have a boat of my own, and give big parties, and go out whenever I like, and watch those gorgeous Players they have at the corner of the streets. I should ask them in whenever I gave an extra big party.

ANNE. I shouldn't. Those Players aren't at all nice people; they're nothing but a lot of ragamuffins, Uncle says, and he has them whipped out of the village when they come near.

ELIZABETH. What a shame! Why? Because they laugh and sing and play, to make people happy?

ANNE. No, because they're not nice people, I tell you. They're rough and they steal, and tell lies and make a horrible noise, and get drunk. . . .

ELIZABETH. Oh, be quiet! How do you know? You've never seen them. I have, once . . . at least, I had a peep at them as we rode past and they didn't look a bit like that. They looked gay, and exciting. I wish I could run away and be a Player.

ANNE. They wouldn't have you because you're a girl. They only have boys as Players.

ELIZABETH. Oh, yes, they would! I should be the first girl Player. I should wear purple velvet, and ride on a horse covered with pearls, and people would rush to the street corners to see me and shout, "Princess Elizabeth, the Famous Player . . . The Player Elizabeth. . . ." (*She sweeps enthusiastically about the stage, dancing and bowing and waving her hand*)

ANNE. Oh, no, you wouldn't. I don't believe they're rich people at all, for all the fine clothes they wear in their plays. If they were rich they wouldn't . . .

ELIZABETH (*interrupting*) Hark! Do you hear something?

ANNE (*in a matter-of-fact voice*) No.

ELIZABETH. Listen. Can't you hear music? And people laughing and singing? (*They listen intently. There comes the sound of men singing and laughing together, a jumble of sound*)

(ANNE *and* ELIZABETH *turn and look at one another. Then* ELIZABETH *runs to the seat on the wall and climbs up on it*)

(*Excitedly*) Anne, come quick!

(ANNE *stands up but does not move forward*)

Who are they? It isn't the . . . yes, it is! Look they're laughing at me, they're laughing. (*She waves her hand excitedly*)

ANNE. Elizabeth, don't, don't! Come back! It's the Players! Don't look at them!

ELIZABETH. They're beckoning to me. I must go out and speak to them.

ANNE (*rushing up to her and catching hold of her gown*) You can't!

ELIZABETH. Perhaps they'd come in here. (*She beckons*) Oh, look, they've stopped!

ANNE (*pulling her back*) You can't. Stop doing that! Aunt Eleanor would be furious.

(ELIZABETH *gets off the seat, and trembling with anger and excitement, pushes Anne firmly into the corner. Then, with tremendous dignity she climbs to the wall again*)

ELIZABETH. Gentlemen, I am the Princess Elizabeth and this is the house of the Countess of Marshlake. She is not here at present, but we both have much pleasure in inviting you to come into our garden.

THE PRINCESS AND THE SWINEHERD

By Nicholas Stuart Gray

Princess Clair-de-Lune, dark and beautiful, but completely spoilt, is the Emperor's daughter. Disguised as a swineheard, Prince Dominic determines to win her and train her to be a docile and useful wife, by teaching her how to live in a ramshackle cottage and keep house for him.

Scene—*A cottage in Aquaraine.*

Period—*1645.*

Dominic. What's gone wrong this time?

Clair-de-Lune. Nothing. Go away.

Dominic. But I've only just come in. I take it there isn't any supper? (*He puts the staff in the corner and the bowls on the table*)

Clair-de-Lune. Everything is burnt black.

Dominic. I can smell that.

Clair-de-Lune. How tiresome you are! It was through no fault of mine. It's the fire! It went out since you last lit it.

Dominic. But that was only an hour ago.

Clair-de-Lune. There's plenty of opportunity for a fire to go out during a whole hour.

Dominic. If it isn't watched.

Clair-de-Lune. I *did* watch it. Only for a moment I forgot it, while I swept the floor. Yes, I did sweep the floor. All over. Exactly as you showed me, with a broom. Only see the pile of dust in the corner there. (*He looks with a faint smile. She stamps her foot*) Don't smile in that irritating way. What have I done wrong this time? I do my best.

Dominic. Are you sure?

Clair-de-Lune. Of course. And if not . . . why should I?

Dominic. Why should you? Perhaps I hoped for too much. (*He turns away, with a sigh. She crosses to him*)

Clair-de-Lune. You've had a good deal more than most swineherds would dare to hope for. A Princess to keep house for you.

Dominic. Well, it's kept me busy, certainly.

Clair-de-Lune. I knew you'd make me angry. While I'm here, I'll trouble you to remember who I am.

Dominic. Have I forgotten?

Clair-de-Lune. You try to make me forget. As though an Emperor's daughter could take any interest in living like a gipsy!

Dominic. Well, you were very bored as a Princess. You might have enjoyed the change.

CLAIR-DE-LUNE. I see nothing to enjoy in hard work.

DOMINIC. Don't you? I always liked doing things . . . and making things. And the harder it was to do, the more fun to succeed. Have you never thought so?

CLAIR-DE-LUNE. Having to do things isn't the same as just thinking them.

DOMINIC. Poor little Princess! And yet your hands look quite capable . . . however small they may be.

CLAIR-DE-LUNE. They look awful. All black and blistered.

DOMINIC. Show me a blister. (*She puts her hands behind her*) Black, possibly . . . you're so silly with fires . . . but I defy you to produce the shadow of a blister. It takes hard work to make a visible one.

CLAIR-DE-LUNE. You're horrid, you are!

DOMINIC. Am I really, Clair-de-Lune?

CLAIR-DE-LUNE. What more can one expect of a swineherd? (*Slight pause. She sits on a stool, head averted*)

DOMINIC. You think a Prince would be gentler company?

CLAIR-DE-LUNE. Naturally.

DOMINIC. How odd!

CLAIR-DE-LUNE. You don't understand my feelings. You expect me to cook and scrub and mend . . . and . . . then feed the hen . . . as though it were my duty. I always thought that peasants had charming lives! I longed to go barefoot and cook eggs, and things. . . .

DOMINIC. But the thought of duty spoils the fun?

CLAIR-DE-LUNE. Of course.

DOMINIC. I suppose it would. After all, I always did these things from choice. But must you think of it as a duty, Princess? Couldn't housekeeping be a game between friends?

CLAIR-DE-LUNE. I'm not your friend.

DOMINIC. Then as a Princess, you should be less silly.

CLAIR-DE-LUNE (*springing up*) What! I beg your pardon!

DOMINIC. You're being horrid to yourself, beg your own. You've stamped on every wish you had to enjoy such freedom as this. You're just waiting for your father to relent, and take you back to court. Aren't you?

CLAIR-DE-LUNE. Well . . . I suppose so.

DOMINIC. And you'll go back a failure . . . even at so simple a task as playing with a doll's house. Have you really grown up no higher than a rattle?

CLAIR-DE-LUNE. You are a pig!

DOMINIC. It comes of tending them.

CLAIR-DE-LUNE. No-one has ever said such things to me!

DOMINIC. No-one can have longed so much to see you happy.

CLAIR-DE-LUNE. Do you?

DOMINIC. Clair-de-Lune, do you dislike me because I am a person you could never love . . . under any circumstances? Or just because I am a swineherd?

CLAIR-DE-LUNE (*disturbed*) I . . . I've no idea what sort of person you may be. Surely it's enough that you *are* a swineherd? How dare you mention the word "love"?

DOMINIC. Because, if you could have loved me, all this would be part of a fairy-tale. Magic greater than any my father's great-aunt knew. Why, a sweeter rose would grow in the garden, and a tenderer nightingale sing through the window. You might have seen a winged horse in the moonlight! And if you'd lived here a peasant all your life . . . you would have felt at last like a Princess.

CLAIR-DE-LUNE. Oh. . . . (*She stiffens*) Impossible nonsense!

DOMINIC. I'm sorry you think it so. Much sorrier for you than myself. Although the month is over, and you will be lost to me, I'll not be bored though I keep pigs for ever . . . but you will go back to Court!

CLAIR-DE-LUNE. You speak as though it would be a misfortune. I want to go back. I'm the Emperor's daughter . . . not a swineherd's wife . . . whatever you choose to think!

DOMINIC. The choice is with you. Until you yourself declare it, you are not really my wife . . . only my Princess.

CLAIR-DE-LUNE. Only?

DOMINIC. Only.

CLAIR-DE-LUNE. Why do you confuse me so? I want to hit you . . . and I want to cry. If we were back at Court, I would have you beaten!

DOMINIC. Would you really, Clair-de-Lune?

CLAIR-DE-LUNE. Try it and see!

DOMINIC. You're hungry, that's what's the matter.

CLAIR-DE-LUNE (*dismally*) It isn't! I don't know why I'm crying. Everything is so disordered and troublesome.

DOMINIC. It might be less disordered if you thought it all less troublesome.

CLAIR-DE-LUNE. Well, I don't, and it is! So what is left?

DOMINIC. Without love, nothing.

CLAIR-DE-LUNE. I've told you not to mention love!

DOMINIC. It was only in passing.

CLAIR-DE-LUNE. Then you should have passed without stopping!

DOMINIC. I won't do it again, Princess. Look, I've raked out the fire. Now I'll relight it, and cook some more oat-cakes for our supper.

CLAIR-DE-LUNE. There isn't any oatmeal.

DOMINIC. There was.

CLAIR-DE-LUNE (*stamping*) Well, there isn't now! I hit the sack with my broom, and it burst . . . and all the meal ran out, and I swept it away to make the floor tidy.

DOMINIC. Then there's nothing to eat. Unless the little hen has laid an egg for you. (*She mumbles something*) I didn't catch that. (*She mumbles again*) Could you make it slightly louder?

CLAIR-DE-LUNE (*shouting*) I trod on it!

DOMINIC. The hen?

CLAIR-DE-LUNE. The egg.

DOMINIC. Oh!

CLAIR-DE-LUNE. I was thinking of something else. I was thinking of something important.

DOMINIC. Well, now I've thought of something. Clair-de-Lune, when do you intend to stop . . . fribbling . . . and start being a Princess? (*She stiffens*) I'm quoting a question that was once put to me, more or less in those very words. But I didn't see the point before. I do, now.

CLAIR-DE-LUNE. I don't.

DOMINIC. For three weeks I've done all the work round here. Cooking, and cleaning, and even the gigantic task of feeding the hen! And you've done nothing. Except sulk, and snap, and wait to go home.

CLAIR-DE-LUNE. How can you be so unkind!

DOMINIC. Because, my Princess, I'll not allow you to go back as a complete and utter failure. What worth is this dignity of yours, if it's based on no competence whatever? What use to fly a banner of pride, if you lower it in the face of every obstacle? If I can't give you love. . . . I'll give you some reason to believe in your own courage. You shall go to market now, and sell these pots I've made.

CLAIR-DE-LUNE. I?

DOMINIC. Well, there's nothing to eat otherwise. I shall be stern, and make you face facts for once in your life.

CLAIR-DE-LUNE. Go to the market . . . I . . . and sell things! I don't know how.

DOMINIC. You'll learn the hard way.

CLAIR-DE-LUNE. You can't force me to!

DOMINIC. Have you so little pride, Princess, that you prefer to be dependent on a swineherd?

CLAIR-DE-LUNE. You shan't taunt me into doing it!

DOMINIC. Then I'll be sterner still. You shall have no food or shelter unless you go, and come back with oatmeal and eggs, having sold the pots.

CLAIR-DE-LUNE. I can't!

DOMINIC. Well, there it is. You must go quickly, too. For the evening is drifting overhead, and the market will soon be done. I'll see to the house, and keep the fire in, till you return. And if you fail to sell the pots, and come empty-handed . . . I shall beat you.

CLAIR-DE-LUNE (*appalled*) Would you really?

DOMINIC. Try it, and see. (*She is not looking at his face, or she could not be taken in for a moment by this threat*)

CLAIR-DE-LUNE. Oh, if my father knew!

DOMINIC. Or mine! Now, off you go to the market . . . or else!

CLAIR-DE-LUNE. You're hateful!

DOMINIC. Perhaps. Here are the pots. Don't break any . . . or else!

CLAIR-DE-LUNE (*taking them*) I'd like to smash them all!

DOMINIC. Well, don't give in to the temptation . . . or else!

CLAIR-DE-LUNE. You stop saying that, at once, or . . .

DOMINIC. Or what?

CLAIR-DE-LUNE (*turning away*) Else. (*She goes to the door, but he calls her, and she stops*)

DOMINIC. Your face is so smudged with tears. Dry your eyes before you go.

(CLAIR-DE-LUNE *sniffs, and tries to do so, but her hands are full of pots.* DOMINIC *goes to her, with great tenderness in his hands and eyes, if not in his words*)

You'll drop everything. Let me do it. (*He smooths his hand across her cheek, but as he has been raking in the ashes he leaves a smear behind*) Oh, I'd forgotten the ashes. How black I've made you look. I'll get some water.

CLAIR-DE-LUNE. Spare yourself the trouble! If I have to go barefoot to market, as a huckster, let me taste the full shame of it, and go with a dirty face! Why pretend to consider my feelings there, when they matter so little to you? (*She turns away but hesitates, and turns back again*) Draw my hair forward, so that it hides my face . . . will you, please? (*He does so and takes off her crown*) Now I must look just like a gipsy. Are you satisfied at last, Swineherd?

(DOMINIC *puts out his hands a little, but she cannot see for her hair. He draws back, and hardens his voice*)

DOMINIC. No, Princess. Not till you return with flying colours.

(CLAIR-DE-LUNE *stamps her foot and nearly drops a pot, which* DOMINIC *retrieves, then she runs out through the door which he has politely opened for her. He stands looking out with the crown in his hands*)

How late it's getting.

THE ROOF

By John Galsworthy

Diana and Bryn Lennox, sisters of thirteen and twelve, are two of many guests staying in an hotel in Paris.

SCENE—*The girls' bedroom in a small hotel.*

TIME—*1929.*

The sisters are having a pillow fight.

DIANA. Pax, Bryn.

BRYN. Pig! You've pulled out three hairs. Look!

DIANA. We can stick them in again. Mum's got some glue. (*She giggles*) Have you wound your watch?

BRYN. No. (*Putting it to her ear*) It's stopped, Di.

DIANA. Put it to twelve. It's striking! Hallo! Listen! Open the door, Bryn.

(BRYN *does*)

I say, isn't it topping? (*They both listen to the violin playing*)

BRYN. Shall I go up and ask him if he'd like us in to hear him? They love audiences, you know. It's all rot when they pretend they don't.

DIANA. You can't in pys.

BRYN. Why not?

DIANA (*grabbing her*) We don't know him.

BRYN. He wouldn't mind, Di.

DIANA. No, Bryn, you can't. Besides I bet he doesn't wash his head.

BRYN. Really!

DIANA. Musicians don't.

BRYN. How do you know?

DIANA. It takes the gloss off. That one at Nauheim never washed —I simply know he didn't.

BRYN. This one washes his ears anyway.

DIANA. He hasn't got any.

BRYN. I saw part of one.

DIANA. Nobody could see through all that hair. You do tell whackers, Bryn.

BRYN (*looking out of the door*) Here he is, Di, coming down. I dare you to ask him if he washes his head.

DIANA. Bryn . . . if you . . . !

88

BRYN. Oh, do come in . . . my sister wants to ask you something.

DIANA (*under her breath; pulls Bryn in*) You little toad!

BRYN. You are a funk, Di. You see, he was quite used to pyjamas. (*She shuts the door*) What can we do now?

DIANA. Yes, I'm not a bit sleepy.

BRYN. I've got a hunch! Those two old things next door—let's tap like the prisoners in Dad's novel . . . the one we're not allowed to read.

DIANA. Now that's what I call sensible. They're stuffy old things!

BRYN. We must do it properly, Di. You say over the alphabet, and I'll do the tapping. (*They crouch on the beds against the wall*) What shall I tap with?

DIANA. I'll get the Dettol bottle. (*She goes to the bathroom*)

BRYN. They always ask each other's names first.

DIANA. Yes, but we know theirs—it's Beeton.

BRYN. Let's start with SOS then.

DIANA. It's an awful strain getting the alphabet right every time. Ready? (*As she says the alphabet over to S* BRYN *taps*) ABCDEFGHIJK-LMNOPQRS. Stop. Now for O. . . . ABCDEFGHIJKLMNO . . .

BRYN. Oh! Di! I overtapped! They got P.

DIANA. Well, what begins with SP?

BRYN. Spot! Sport! Spillikins!

DIANA. I know. Starting Price! Only that doesn't seem to lead to anything. We'll have to begin again. Let's try: Are you there? . . . A . . .

(BRYN *taps once*)

Now R . . . ABCD. (*Knocks from next door*) It sounds as if they didn't like it. (*Giggle*)

BRYN. I don't expect they were ever in prison. They don't look sports. Shall we try again?

DIANA. No. It's too risky.

BRYN. Well, we must do something.

DIANA. I tell you what . . . There are some honeyspooners in the room opposite.

BRYN. How do you know they're honeyspooners?

DIANA. I watched them at dinner. Their eyes were all swimmy. Disgusting! We might give them a lesson. They're only French.

BRYN. They're not. If you mean the girl with all that neck.

DIANA. Well! They were speaking French with an awful lot of accent.

BRYN. Only showing off. I heard the man say "damn" in the hall.

DIANA (*doubtfully*) Oh! That makes a difference. They might cut up rusty.

BRYN. Well, let's only put on hats and coats and run in as if we thought it was our room.

DIANA. Yes, that's quite natural.

BRYN. Only . . . the door'll be locked, Di.

DIANA. It mightn't be—yet.

BRYN. Honeyspooners always lock their doors the first minute.

DIANA. How do you know?

BRYN. Because the moment they get in, he says, "Darlin'!" and she says, "Oh, James!" and then they kiss. W-whew!

DIANA. Bryn, you're awful!

BRYN. I know! Let's stand outside their door and miaow!

DIANA. That's a good idea.

BRYN. You do it, Di. And I'll watch when they come out.

DIANA. You are a worm!

BRYN. Well, bag's last.

DIANA. We'd better rehearse. You spit best . . . you do the spitting. (*They rehearse softly*)

BRYN. All right.

DIANA. Begin low, Bryn, and rather *rallentando*, then we'll work up! Now!

They begin. As the caterwauling builds up, they exit.

THE SEA KING'S DAUGHTER

By Margaret Harding

A group of children put on a play: Princess Marina is lured away from the palace by the green-eyed Sea Serpent, who pretends that Marina can save an attack on her father's kingdom by coming to the enemy; the Octopus.

SCENE—*A part of the ocean.*

TIME—*The present.*

After a few moments the SERPENT *enters* R, *dragging* MARINA *after her.* MARINA *is crying and struggles to free herself.*

SERPENT. It's useless to cry out for help now, my fine Princess. No-one can hear you, the Palace is many miles behind us. Here there is nothing but the wild barren ocean. Listen to the storm. Isn't it glorious? Your feeble little voice is lost in its mighty sound. Listen, Marina, and fear; this is the only real King of the Sea—and he speaks in a voice of thunder—all who live beneath the sea and those who sail above us know and dread this voice.

MARINA. Have pity. Let me return to my father.

SERPENT. Look about you. This is the real ocean, desolate, cruel. You have never been beyond the quiet gardens of the palace, have you, Marina? There it is always calm, isn't it? The lazy waters gently lap the fronds of seaweed, and all the year round the flowers are brilliant—never withering.

MARINA. Take me back. I am afraid here, it is so dark and evil.

(The SERPENT *drags Marina by her hair to* C)

Oh, you hurt me—my hair.

SERPENT. You should not have such beautiful long hair, Princess —it may become entangled in the rocks as we climb to the fortress of the Octopus. I should hate to see you lose that lovely hair, I envy it so.

MARINA. You are cruel beyond relief. As cruel as this dim kingdom through which we pass. I can do nothing, nothing only try not to show my fear.

SERPENT. Come, then, the Octopus does not like to be kept waiting. The most difficult part of our journey still lies ahead of us. You will see many strange sights yet before we reach our destination. See—(*she points* L) that is our pathway.

MARINA (*looking off* L) Not that narrow little ledge that winds up the sides of the steep chasm?

SERPENT. Yes, it is narrow, isn't it? One slip and you sink down and down deeper than the ocean bed itself—none have ever returned from the bottomless chasm. But we shall make our way along that ledge until we come to the fortress. You have nothing to fear, you will be quite safe with me.

(*The* DOLPHIN *stirs and moans.* MARINA *and the* SERPENT *see her.* MARINA, *with a quick movement, slips out of the Serpent's hold and runs to the Dolphin*)

MARINA. Why, it is the wise Dolphin. How did she come . . . ?

SERPENT (*crossing to Marina and dragging her* C) You little fool—do not try to escape me like that again, or I shall not be so gentle with you. Who is this old creature huddled here? She looks half dead.

MARINA (*struggling*) But it is my dear Wise Dolphin. She must have come to search for me and have been overcome by the storm. Oh, let me try to help her, please.

SERPENT (*fearing pursuit*) No, we cannot stay here longer. We already have a long way to go and the storm will delay us as it is.

MARINA. One moment, please. Then do what you like—take me where you will. I cannot leave her to die.

SERPENT (*dragging Marina* L) I say no, and you will obey me. Come, you have a dangerous journey before you, my little one.

THE SECRET GARDEN

By Frances Hodgson-Burnett
adapted from the novel

Mary Lennox, aged ten, has lived in her uncle's great, lonely house on the Yorkshire Moors, since her parents died in India. She and Dickon, a country lad, have found a secret garden, and Mary has discovered that she has a cousin, Colin, a boy, her own age, and as pale, unhealthy and disagreeable as she herself had once been.

SCENE—*Night-time in Colin's bedroom.*

TIME—*1911.*

COLIN *is having a tantrum, and screaming in the night.* MARY *goes to his room.*

MARY (*outside the room, listening*) It's Colin. He's having one of those tantrums the nurse calls hysterics. How awful it sounds. (*She shivers*) I don't know what to do. I don't know what to do. I can't bear it. He ought to be stopped . . . somebody ought to make him stop. (*She runs in to Colin's room, angrily*) You stop! You stop! I hate you. Everybody hates you! I wish everybody would run out of the house and let you scream yourself to death! You will scream yourself to death in a minute and I wish you would!

(COLIN *turns on his pillow, gasping and choking*)

If you scream another scream, I'll scream too—and I can scream louder than you can, and I'll frighten you—I'll frighten you.

COLIN (*choking*) I can't stop! I can't . . . I can't!

MARY (*shouting*) You can! Half that ails you is hysterics . . . and temper! Just hysterics—hysterics . . . hysterics! (*Stamping her foot*)

COLIN. I felt the lump . . . I felt it! I knew I should! I shall have a hunch on my back and then I shall die! (*He turns on his face and sobs and wails*)

MARY (*fiercely*) You didn't feel a lump! If you did it was only a hysterical lump. Hysterics makes lumps. There's nothing the matter with your horrid back—nothing but hysterics! Turn over and let me look at it. . . .

(COLIN *slowly turns, and* MARY *inspects his back*)

There's not a single lump there! There's not a lump as big as a pin —except backbone lumps, and you can only feel them because you're thin. I've got backbone lumps myself, and they used to stick out as much as yours do, until I began to get fatter, and I am not fat enough yet to hide them. There's not a lump as big as a pin. If you ever say there is again, I shall laugh! There!

COLIN (*sobs for a while, then turns*) Do—you—think I—could—live—to grow up?

MARY. You probably will if you do what you are told to do, and not give way to your temper, and stay out a good deal in the fresh air.

(COLIN *reaches for* MARY's *hand. She is calmer and takes it*)

COLIN. I'll—I'll go out with you, Mary. I shan't hate fresh air if we can find the secret garden. I shall like to go out with you if Dickon will come and push my chair. I do so want to see Dickon and the fox and the crow.

MARY. Would you like me to sing that song I learned from my ayah?

COLIN. Oh, yes, it's such a soft song. I shall go to sleep in a minute. I won't talk and I'll go to sleep, but you said you had a whole lot of nice things to tell me. Have you . . . do you think you have found out anything at all about the way into the secret garden?

MARY. Ye-es, I think I have. And if you will go to sleep I will tell you tomorrow.

COLIN (*trembling*) O Mary! O Mary! If I could get into it I think I should live to grow up! Do you suppose that instead of singing the Ayah song—you could just tell me softly as you did that first day what you imagine it looks inside? I am sure it will make me go to sleep.

MARY. Yes. Shut your eyes.

(COLIN *closes his eyes and* MARY *holds his hand and speaks softly*)

I think that it has been left alone so long that it has grown all into a lovely tangle. I think the roses have climbed and climbed and climbed until they hang from the branches and walls and creep over the ground—almost like a strange grey mist. Some of them have died . . . but many are alive, and when the summer comes there will be curtains and fountains of roses. I think the ground is full of daffodils and snowdrops and lilies and iris working their way out of the dark. Now the spring has begun perhaps . . . perhaps . . . perhaps they are coming up through the grass—perhaps there are clusters of purple crocuses and gold ones—even now. Perhaps the leaves are beginning to break out and uncurl . . . and perhaps—the grey is changing and a green gauze veil is creeping and creeping over—everything. And the birds are coming to look at it—because it is . . . so safe and still. And perhaps . . . perhaps . . . perhaps (*slowly and softly*) the robin has found a mate . . . and is building his nest.

And COLIN *is asleep.*

THE SILVER ROSE

By J. C. Trewin

Grand Duchess Anna hid the diamonds of San Leon when her father died. Her cousins, leading a rebellion against Anna, visit her in the old nursery where she is imprisoned with the maid Juanita.

SCENE—*Anna's nursery in the Palace at San Leon.*

TIME—*Mid-nineteenth century.*

The bolts of the door rattle. The WARDER *enters, ushering in the* LADY FLORA CALVAS. *She is sixteen, the same age as the Grand Duchess, an imperious girl in a white cloak. She inclines her head very slightly when she enters and then jerks it up again as if she has made an error.*

FLORA (*to Warder*) You may leave us. (*To Anna*) Senorita Falerna, is it not? Did you expect me?

ANNA. Not so early in the morning, Flora. You were a lazy child.

FLORA (*sitting*) It's a nice room, this nursery of yours. You were always at home in a nursery.

ANNA. You should know the room well enough.

FLORA. No rocking-horse now? No dolls?

ANNA. I'm afraid, Flora, we have no time to play.

FLORA. Then we had better go straight to the point.

ANNA. By all means.

FLORA. Ten days ago you ruled San Leon, the youngest ruler in Europe, the girl Grand Duchess. It was not your fault your father died . . .

ANNA. Thank you.

FLORA. But you can hardly say your reign was successful. Six months and then a rebellion.

ANNA. As you say—then a rebellion.

FLORA. Uncle Michael should never have been Protector. A stupid little man. You were under age; you had no right to succeed.

ANNA. Merely the right of my father's daughter.

FLORA. And now my brother has what he deserved six months ago.

ANNA. You can hardly expect me to agree with you.

FLORA. Who cares for that? The work is nearly over, my dear. My father's troops have taken San Leon. We have taken Uncle Michael. We have taken *you*. (*Sharply*) Everything—and at our command.

ANNA. Everything, you say?

FLORA. Everything. We command the mountains, the plain, the river. . . .

ANNA. And the people?

FLORA. Naturally.

ANNA. I don't believe it.

FLORA. But you *must* believe it. It may be hard for you, Anna, I don't deny that—a girl brought so young to so great a duty. Why are you stubborn? If you had trusted my brother, he would have helped you.

ANNA. He has. We are back to the nursery. Everything but pinafores.

FLORA. And nothing at all to do. Even the rocking-horse doesn't work. And (*laughs*) that doll by your bed!

ANNA. Old friends, Flora.

FLORA. It's your own fault that we're enemies. (*Urgently*) My brother has sent me to you.

ANNA. For company? Thank you, I have Juanita.

FLORA. Don't be foolish. All this week my brother—Conrad—has asked you one question. One question.

ANNA. I am quite used to it.

FLORA. Where have you hidden the diamonds of San Leon? The diamonds of San Leon—the wealth of the Grand Duchy. Need I tell *you* that they pass from ruler to ruler? The Chamberlain stutters and stammers. No-one has seen them since your father died. Six months ago, Anna. We know you must have hidden them. . . . Then where are they hidden? Tell us now, and my brother may let you go.

ANNA. Where?

FLORA. How should I know? Exile.

ANNA. To Alban?

FLORA. I dare say.

ANNA (*gently*) It is kind of him—but I choose my own time to go.

FLORA (*angrily*) Understand your position, Anna. You are alone, you are friendless. You cannot leave this palace. For you it's nothing but a prison. And you will stay in it here—in your nursery—a child without her toys, a child in the corner—until you see reason.

ANNA. Reason! You call it that—to give up my own to the first highwayman.

FLORA. So! You *have* the diamonds.

ANNA. I have not said it.

FLORA. Conrad told me you were stubborn. But didn't I know it! He never played with you!

ANNA. Played against me would be better. . . . Try to be gentler, Flora, it might pay. You want something. Then you ought to wheedle and stroke.

FLORA. I shall speak my mind.

ANNA. Flora, say this to your brother. The Grand Duchess of San Leon does not yield to force. Not even his force. All that was entrusted to me I shall keep.

FLORA. You will hear more.

ANNA. That will hardly surprise me.

FLORA (*imperiously*) Warder!

(*The* WARDER *enters*)

FLORA. I am ready to go. Conduct me to the gate.

WARDER. Your pardon my lady, the Duke has sent a message. He will be here to meet you. Will you please to wait for him in the farther hall?

FLORA. Take me there. (*To Anna*) You see! . . . You see!

FLORA *and the* WARDER *go out.*

THE SNOW QUEEN

By Suria Magito and Rudolf Weil

Gerda, a little Danish girl, is seeking for her friend, a boy, Kay, who has been taken by the Snow Queen. On her long journey, Gerda meets Karl, a raven, and has many adventures before finding Kay in the Queen's Palace.

SCENE: *The road to the North.*

(GERDA *comes in, tramping wearily and carrying a small bundle. She is humming the organ-grinder's tune*)

GERDA. Everywhere I go I find the roads the same and the people strange. . . . . Oh! (*Stopping*) I wonder how many days, how many weeks, how many months I have travelled now? The snow had just gone when I left home. Then came the spring and the flowers, and the sun got hotter and hotter, till the summer came and the dust. The leaves are falling about me now, so it must be autumn and . . . Oh! (*Realizing it*) It will soon be winter again and I still have not found Kay. Must I search all through the cold winter too? (*She weeps a little and sits*) Now I know what it is to be really alone. All alone! (*Looking round, sighs*)

(*Suddenly a raven*—KARL *appears. She does not see him and he does not see her. He crows to himself*)

KARL. Kra!—kra!

(GERDA *screams and jumps up. At her scream* KARL *screeches and flaps a good foot into the air. They both stand apart, facing and unsure of each other*)

GERDA (*timidly*) Good . . . afternoon . . . Mr . . . Raven.
KARL (*timidly*) Good . . . afternoon . . . madam . . . or miss. (*Silence as they eye each other*) You aren't going to grasp for a branch and thrash me?
GERDA. Why, no, sir.
KARL. Nor cast a sharp stone at my back?
GERDA. No, sir.
KARL: Nor your parcel?
GERDA. Oh, no, sir.
KARL. Ah! (*Relieved*) Grand! Grand! You are marvellously well brought-up! Maaarvellously! Don't I talk grandly?
GERDA. You do indeed.
KARL. Hahaha! Passing my young days in the castle park—I learned

98

the jargon of the court. I am half a court raven. But Klara is a court raven in fact!

GERDA. Klara? But who is that?

KARL. Klara is my bride to be. She gets her nourishment from the royal larder, real royal garbage, you understand?

GERDA. Yes, I see, sir.

KARL. You aren't from these parts—or are you?

GERDA (sighing) No, sir, I come from very far away.

KARL. Far parts—far parts—I took it for granted. Is that why you are so downhearted?

GERDA. No, it's because I can't find my friend whom I am looking for—everywhere—a boy.

KARL. A lad? Ah! Can I help you? I'm a past master in helping!

GERDA. Thank you. Oh, if you only could. You see, we lived together so happily—he and Granny and I. But one day, last winter, the Snow Queen came and fetched him—and he has never been seen again. The name of the boy is . . .

KARL (quickly) Kay?

GERDA. How do you know?

KARL. And you are Gerda?

GERDA. Yes, I am called Gerda. But how . . . ?

KARL. Haha! Our aunt, the magpie, a ghastly gossip, knows all that passes in the far world!

GERDA. Then you . . . you know where Kay is? Answer me! Quick!

KARL. Kra-ra! Kra-ra! For forty days we asked and guessed, discussed and examined the facts——

GERDA. And?

KARL. —tried to establish, to learn, to discover where he had vanished to——

GERDA. And?

KARL. —to detect his moves, to track them, to check them——

GERDA. And?

KARL. —to . . . to . . . to . . .

GERDA. And?

KARL. Not a chance of a glance!

GERDA (disappointed) Oh . . . !

KARL. Hark!

GERDA. What's the matter?

KARL. Hark! Hark! That's Klara! That charming flapping of her wings. Grand! (A second raven appears) Darling Klara!

THE TINDER BOX

By Nicholas Stuart Gray

The King has imprisoned his daughter, Gisella, because a fortune-teller has prophesied that she will marry a soldier. The witch, disguised as a lady-in-waiting to the Princess, is determined to find the magic tinder-box.

SCENE—*The Princess' room in the tower.*

TIME—*Sixteenth century.*

PRINCESS GISELLA *sits on the stool by the bed, reading.*

GISELLA. How lovely the snow is . . . falling so quietly. I wish I could feel its cold feathers against my cheeks. I wish it could talk to me . . . good evening, snow. . . . I've been reading about you in my book. A poem about your white feathers. How odd that I may only read of things, now, and never really know them for myself again. How sad, that I shall stay imprisoned in this tower until I die. But I won't think about that . . . it will make my head ache. I'll read some more about the snow, and not look where it is falling over all the people who are free to enjoy it. . . . (*She runs back to her stool, to read in her book again*)

> . . . . know henceforth
> It's the shedding of their feathers
> By the Snow-birds of the North.

(*The* WITCH *enters,* R, *through the arch. She curtsies, and the* PRINCESS *goes on reading*)

WITCH. It's me, Princess!

(*She waves her hand archly, as the* PRINCESS *starts up with a cry, dropping her book, and backing away*)

Now what's the matter? You're always jumping when I come in. You're not frightened of me, are you? Your nice new lady-in-waiting?

GISELLA. I am rather frightened of you, I think. I don't know why. None of my other ladies frighten me.

WITCH. How unkind you are. And me so fond of you, even in the short week that I've been attending you. I did hope you would grow to love me . . . and now you say things like that . . . oh! . . .

(*She pretends to cry, and the* PRINCESS *goes to her with reluctant sympathy*)

GISELLA. Please don't cry. I shouldn't have said it, I suppose. Forgive me. My behaviour must seem very strange to you, but remember I have been a prisoner in this tower since I was fifteen . . . for three endless years . . . you'd overlook my stupidity when you think of that, wouldn't you?

WITCH. Yes, yes, but you must try to love me, and trust me. Now don't say you can't trust me!

GISELLA. Well . . . I *will* try.

WITCH. That's a good girl. You behave nicely, and perhaps your father will let you out.

GISELLA. He won't. Not ever. Once Father gets an idea into his head, it sticks like a burr. He thinks it would be unkingly to change his mind.

WITCH. Can't your mother do anything to help you?

GISELLA. She can't cope with Father at all. She says she's given up. So here I am, and here I must stay. All because of a fortune-teller and his foolish tongue.

WITCH. I wondered why you should be imprisoned here. I can't imagine that you've done anything really wrong. You haven't the . . . I mean, you're not the type, dear Princess Gisella.

GISELLA. I'd rather not talk about it. It makes my head ache.

WITCH. That's with reading so much.

GISELLA (*passionately*) What else is there for me to do? Other girls may dance, and ride, and play . . . but they are not in prison! I can never pick flowers or feed the swans on the lake . . . or stop my horse to speak with children by the road-side! I must only look out of this one window over the roofs of the town and over the trees, and beyond. And everything that exists . . . in the town, or the forests, or the sea . . . I must read about in books, or forget altogether. And all because my father thinks a king must have everything as he wishes it . . . and because a fortune-teller said I would marry a soldier!

WITCH. A what?

GISELLA. A soldier . . . a common, ordinary soldier!

WITCH. Well, I never. Your father was quite right to take no risks about that. I hate soldiers!

GISELLA. I've never met one. Why did you make me speak about it? I shall never sleep tonight.

WITCH. Well, you'd better try. Let me unfasten your pretty gown.

(*The* PRINCESS *backs away from her*)

Now come, my dear. Don't you trust Witchy . . . I mean Nursey?

GISELLA. I'm sorry, but . . . I'd rather you didn't touch me. I'll change for bed without your help . . . in my other room. . . .

(*She runs out,* R. *The* WITCH *shrugs her shoulders*)

WITCH. She doesn't like me. Odd little thing! Oh, well. Everything else is going very nicely. The slaves are on the job now, searching the town for a wounded penniless soldier . . . how they hated being sent out in the snow! Ha, serve them right, lazy things. And I'm here, all warm and cosy, and waiting for news. It won't be long before they find him. (*She goes to the spinning-wheel, and moves some books down from the stool. She sits there, and starts spinning*) Hmm . . . hmm . . . hmm . . .

> (*She starts to sing*)
>
> Spin, spin, spin, spin,
> Up and down and out and in, . .
>
> (*She waves her hand over the* SPINNING-WHEEL)

Come along, wheel dear, you sing a little, too. Make a pretty noise for Auntie.

> (*A quiet little tune emanates from the* SPINNING-WHEEL *as it turns, and the* WITCH *sings*)
>
> Spinning makes me feel so gay
> I could spin all night and day,
> Hmm . . . hmm . . . hmm . . .
> Here I sit and watch my wheel
> All dressed-up and most genteel,
> Spinning thread without a hitch,
> No-one guesses I'm a WITCH!
> Wow!
>
> (*She pricks her finger, and stops spinning to suck it frantically*)

Poor finger! You can just stop that noise, you nasty dangerous thing, you!

> (*The* SPINNING-WHEEL *stops its tune. The* WITCH *binds her finger with her handkerchief*)

There ought to be a notice on spinning-wheels saying "dangerous". My mother told me that once a girl pricked her finger on one and went to sleep for a hundred years. Now, that's what I call going too far. I'd like to send the Princess to sleep for a hundred years. Hm. Wonder if I could? No. Must stick to one thing at a time. Dangerous to change your mind at this time of year. I'd like to send for my slaves and see how they're getting on, but it wouldn't do for the Princess to find her lady-in-waiting messing about with magic. I told you to be quiet!

> (*This is to the* SPINNING-WHEEL, *which has started its little tune again. It stops immediately.*)
>
> *The* PRINCESS *enters, in a long white night-robe, with her long hair loose on her shoulders*)

Just in time!
GISELLA. What did you say, Madam Mommet?
WITCH. I said "just in time". Just in time to say good night to

me before I go. I've been asked to accompany the King and Queen, and other members of the Court to a banquet tonight, at the house of a rich new-comer to the town. I shall enjoy myself. Haven't been to a banquet for years.

GISELLA. Nor I.

WITCH. You're safer here. Now into bed with you, and give your kind lady-in-waiting a kiss.

GISELLA. I . . . I'd rather not. (*She picks up a book and gets into bed*)

WITCH. You'll go cross-eyed, reading in this light.

GISELLA. I shan't sleep tonight, unless I forget my own thoughts in someone else's. Forgive me, if I've been rude to you, Madam Mommet. I'm always nervous with strangers, now. I won't read too late. Can't you put a spell on me to make me sleep?

WITCH. What d'you think I am? A witch?

GISELLA (*laughing*) I was joking. Enjoy your banquet.

WITCH. Phew! Good night, Princess. I'll be off. I must have a word with a couple of servants of mine. . . .

(*The heads of* KUFUFFLE *and* SHEMOZZLE *emerge from under the Princess's bed. The* WITCH *stares at them in amazement and fury, and makes frantic gestures for caution.* GISELLA *is looking out of the window, and does not see them*)

Psst! Outside! Really! My nerves!

(*The* SLAVES *scamper off, and the* WITCH *puts her hand to her head, and chases after them.* GISELLA *reads from her book, sighing*)

GISELLA.   Sun and stars are free to wander
                  Under all eternity . . .
                  Who will set me free, I wonder?
                  Or must I die?

THE WASHERWOMAN'S CHILD

By Alison Uttley

Seven of Hans Andersen's famous tales are dramatized in this play linked with scenes from the author's own life. In the story of the Snow Queen, Gerda, a little Danish girl, loses her friend Kay, when the Queen takes him; but after many adventures, she finds him again.

Scene—*A street in Odense.*

GERDA. Hello, Kay. Look at the snow!

KAY. Hello, Gerda. Isn't it lovely! My grandmother says it's white bees swarming. They've come out of their hive in the sky.

GERDA. My grandmother says it's the Snow Queen up there. She flies in the clouds and breathes with her frosty breath on the windows, and then the beautiful strange flowers come. She makes the frost gardens.

KAY. The Snow Queen? If I saw the Snow Queen I would put her on the stove and melt her.

GERDA. Look, Kay. The snow has killed our roses on our little trees. Look how they hang, with petals withered.

KAY. Yes, it's the Snow Queen's icy fingers that have done it. Oh!

GERDA. Kay, you will always like me, won't you? You'll always be my friend?

KAY. Of course, Gerda. We'll go sledging this afternoon after we have gathered firewood for our grandmothers. Would you like that?

GERDA. Yes, Kay. Then you shall come home to tea with me and we'll look at my new book. It's my godmother's present to me. (*She holds up a large, gay book*)

KAY. Oh. That will be grand, Gerda.

(*The* MAGICIAN *glides across the stage, waving the mirror at them. He drops it, and it shatters. He laughs, and hurries away*)

KAY (*giving a little cry*) Ah! What was that shooting pain in my eye? Oh! Something has hurt my heart. Oh, the pain!

GERDA (*running to him*) Darling Kay! What's the matter?

KAY. Nothing. It's gone. (*He pushes her away roughly, so that she falls*) Don't fuss. You are an ugly girl. Get away, I detest you.

GERDA. Kay! (*She takes out her handkerchief and weeps silently*)

KAY. You are even uglier when you cry. Look at this old rose tree. Horrid old dead thing. (*He kicks it, and struts about, banging and*

104

smashing) Look at your old picture book. It's a baby's book. I don't want it. (*He snatches it and throws it away*)

GERDA (*staring at him and faltering*) Are you going sledging with me, Kay?

KAY. No, indeed! I'm going with some boys. Grown-up boys. I'm going to sledge as I please. (*He gets his scarlet sledge from the gable house and stands there in the snow*)

GERDA *enters the house and shuts the door.*

THE WASHERWOMAN'S CHILD

SCENE—*The Palace of the Snow Queen.*

GERDA (*running forward*) Kay! Kay! I have found you at last.

(KAY *takes no notice, but keeps on arranging the splinters*)

(*Putting her arms around him*) Kay, beloved Kay! It's Gerda, come to find you and take you home.

(KAY *ignores her and she weeps. Her hot tears touch his breast as he stands like a stone, and the splinter from the Magician's mirror is melted*)

KAY. Oh! Something has gone from my heart. Gerda! My friend Gerda! Where have you been all this time? Where am I? What is this place? How cold it is, here, how wide and empty and terrible.

GERDA. Oh, how glad I am to find you, Kay! You are at the World's End, and I have found you. (*She kisses him, and they fling their arms around each other. The ice maidens cover their faces, and move away. A bright light from heaven shines on the two*)

GERDA. What is this game you are playing, Kay? What are these letters?

KAY. I'm trying to make a word, and it won't be made.

GERDA. Why, here it is. ETERNITY. (*She hangs the word on the icicle spikes. The letters must be rough, with jagged icy points*)

KAY. ETERNITY! That's what I've been seeking, all this time. The Snow Queen said I could be my own master when I found the word. She said I could have the whole world, and a pair of skates, too.

GERDA. Well, the whole world is thine, Kay, and here is the pair of skates. (*She picks up a pair from among the icicles*) You can be your own master and come away with me. The Reindeer is waiting for us, and soon we shall be home again.

KAY. I remember—I remember—a rose tree, and the house where I was born.

GERDA. Come away now, Kay. It is all waiting for us, home, and the rose tree.

KAY. I remember something else, Gerda. I remember that I love thee.

GERDA. And I love thee, Kay. (*They kiss*) Now, come with me. We will call to see the Wise Woman in her hut, and the Robber Maid with her dagger, and the Prince and Princess who helped me, and the Raven who talked Ravenish to me. They will all be glad to see us. Then we will cross the forests and find the river, and go home to the little house in Denmark.

KAY. And I will never leave thee again, dear Gerda.

They walk back to the little bush, where the Reindeer is waiting with the sledge. GERDA *sits in the sledge, and* KAY *runs by her side, as the Reindeer draws her off.*

THE WEAVER OF RAVELOE

By Eric Jones-Evans
From the novel *Silas Marner* by George Eliot

Eppie is nineteen and the adopted daughter of Silas Marner; Aaron is twenty-three and the son of Dolly Winthrop, housekeeper to the Squire, and kind friend to Silas.

Scene—*Silas Marner's cottage.*

Time—*1821.*

Eppie (*at the door*) Why, Aaron, 'tis you! Come in.

(Aaron, *carrying a nosegay of flowers, enters*)

Aaron. Sure I'm not intrudin', Eppie?

Eppie. O' course not. Come in, an' sit down. Father's gone for a bit of a walk.

Aaron. I know. I met him in the lane. He told me to come on up.

Eppie (*clearing the table*) What brings you here this time o' day?

Aaron (*handing her the nosegay*) This—for one thing.

Eppie (*taking it*) Oh, thank you, Aaron! Thank you! They are pretty. (*She smells flowers rapturously*)

Aaron. An' I—I've some news for ye too, Eppie. Good news.

Eppie. What is it?

Aaron. Ye know 'ow kind Mr Godfrey's been to us arl, since the old Squire died seven years back?

Eppie. Yes.

Aaron (*eagerly*) Well, old Martin's rheumatism's got so bad, 'e's been obliged to give up 'is job at the Red 'Ouse gardens. So, today, Mr Godfrey pensioned 'im off.

Eppie. Well?

Aaron. This'll surprise you, Eppie! I—I've got 'is place.

Eppie (*amazed*) What! Mr Godfrey's never made ye second gardener?

Aaron. 'E 'as. An' raised my wages, too.

Eppie. How wonderful!

Aaron. That's why I've come to see ye, Eppie. I—I want to ask ye a question.

Eppie (*timidly*) What—what is it ye want to know, Aaron?

Aaron (*earnestly*) When you're goin' to marry me. There's naught to stop us, my dear, now I've got this situation. Mr Godfrey's promised me a cottage, an' I can make a pretty little 'ome for ye. So—tell me ye'll wed me soon.

EPPIE. But—but, Aaron, I—I've never given it a thought.

AARON. Then 'tis time ye did, my love.

EPPIE. I—I don't know what to say.

AARON (*taking her gently in his arms*) No need to say anythin'—only that ye love me—an' ye'll marry me.

EPPIE. I—I do love you, Aaron. I told ye so last time ye asked me. But—as for marryin' . . .

AARON. Well?

EPPIE. Why d'ye want us to be wed in such a hurry?

AARON. Because I'm twenty-three years o' age, Eppie, an' love ye more than life itself.

EPPIE. But—but Aaron . . .

AARON. You're not frightened, are ye?

EPPIE. No, no—of course not.

AARON. Then make up your mind, Eppie. Everybody's married sometime.

EPPIE. That's not true, Aaron.

AARON. What d'ye mean?

EPPIE. Father wasn't married. He was a lone man till I was sent to him. An' that's another thing—if I did marry you, I could never, never leave him on his own.

AARON. Ye wouldn't 'ave to, Eppie. I should never dream o' takin' ye away from 'im.

EPPIE (*earnestly*) It'd be no use if ye did.

AARON. 'E can come an' live wi' us, my dear. There'll be plenty o' room at the cottage. Then 'e needn't work at all—only what's for 'is own pleasure—an' I'd be as good as a son to 'im, I would indeed.

EPPIE. But—but we're very happy as we are. I don't want a change—leastways, not at present.

AARON (*sadly*) That means, then, you—you don't care for me at all.

EPPIE. Yes, yes, I do—indeed, I do, Aaron. But why can't we go on as we are?

AARON (*hurt*) I've already told ye. 'Tis cruel o' ye to play the fool wi' me like this, Eppie. If ye cared for me the least little bit, ye'd want us to be married, as I do.

EPPIE (*sobbing a little*) Oh, don't be unkind, Aaron. I'm so very, very fond of you. There's no-one I love better—except father.

AARON (*cutting in*) They why . . .

EPPIE (*drying her eyes*) 'Tis because I don't want anything to change—not for a little while, at any rate. Oh, Aaron, let's go on being happy as we are.

AARON (*after a pause*) All right, my dear. But will ye promise to think it over?

EPPIE (*smiling up at him*) Yes, yes, I will, indeed. And I'll talk to father as well. I wouldn't do anything without first tellin' him. Ye do understand, don't you?

AARON. O' course I do. I *I'm*—sorry if I spoke roughly to ye just now. 'Twas because I—I love ye so, and . . .

(SILAS *passes the window*)

EPPIE. Say no more about it. (*She hears the click of the latch*) Hush! Here's Father now.

THE WISHING WELL

By Mabel Constanduros

Mary is a little girl. Suzanne is older and less timid.

SCENE—*By a wishing well.*

TIME—*The present.*

SUZANNE (*recovering*) Gracious! You did give me a start. I thought you were the ghost.

MARY. It—it *is* haunted, then?

SUZANNE. So they say—by Saint Phayre who drowned herself in the well because they wouldn't let her be a nun. But I don't believe in ghosts, do you?

MARY. I don't know . . .

SUZANNE. Have you come to wish?

MARY. Yes. They don't know at home. They think I'm in bed.

SUZANNE. They think I am, too. At least, I hope so. I shall get into the most frightful row if they find out. I hope we shan't have to wait long.

MARY. Till the moonbeam strikes the well, isn't it?

SUZANNE. Yes. On Midsummer Eve. And if you dip your fingers in the water and call on St Phayre in the proper words your wish'll come true.

MARY. Oh, I do hope mine will.

SUZANNE. Mine's jolly well got to. I'm going to wish they'd let me go on the stage. My aunt's so ridiculous about it, you can't think. Narrow-minded isn't the word. She won't even let me do acrobatic dancing—says it isn't "lady-like", if you ever heard such nonsense. What are you going to wish?

MARY. I'm going to wish Mummy and Daddy'll come back from India so that I needn't go to boarding-school any more. I shall be in Miss Wotherspoon's form next term and she's such a pig I feel I simply *can't* bear it.

SUZANNE. They *can* be pigs, too—don't I know it? My aunt's the hampering kind—*you* know. Won't let you do a *thing* you want to. Hamper, hamper, hamper till you feel you could be rude.

MARY. Yes, and if you are, the fuss they make! Even if they've *goaded* you to it.

SUZANNE. I can't think what makes people behave like that to children. I'm sure I shan't when I'm grown up.

MARY. They don't mean to be horrid—they just don't think.

SUZANNE. *Won't* think, you mean.

MARY. Oh, I don't know. I spend my holidays with my grandmother. She's quite sweet in her way, but she thinks I ought to be contented to play with dolls all day and read "Jessica's First Prayer" and "Queechy" in the evenings. She won't let me have anyone in to tea for fear they'll "upset the maids", or tread on the rose-beds—tread on the rose-beds, I ask you!

SUZANNE. And I suppose you're never allowed to go to the flicks in case you "catch something". Don't I know! You wait till I'm doing pictures myself! As soon as *ever* I've left school I shall go *straight* to Hollywood—I shan't wait a moment.

MARY. It's almost time. The moonbeam's nearly got to the well.

SUZANNE. I tell you what. If we both wished the same wish wouldn't that make it more certain to come true?

MARY. But we don't want the same thing. Listen! Was that someone coming?

SUZANNE. No. Don't get so panicky. Let's see if we couldn't make one wish do.

MARY. Isn't it maddening to think that if we were only grown up we could do as we liked and we needn't creep here in the dark and wait for the moon to shine on the well? We could stop at home and just *make* whatever we wanted happen.

SUZANNE. That's it. You've got it.

MARY. Got what?

SUZANNE. Don't you see, if we wished that children had all the power that grown-ups have and grown-ups had to do as children told them we shouldn't *have* all this bother. We could do as we liked.

MARY. Oo! Fancy me bossing Miss Wotherspoon about and telling her not to forget herself—like she does me.

SUZANNE. And fancy me sending Aunt Hester to bed at half past seven and telling her to stand up straight every minute of her life. Oh, let's do it!

MARY. All right. We must be quick and think what to say. The beam's nearly got to the well.

SUZANNE. First we have to say the rhyme.

MARY. Yes.

> With my finger in your well,
> Good Saint Phayre my wish I tell. . . .

SUZANNE. Then we'll say both together, "We wish that children and grown-ups could change places."

MARY. What do we do afterwards?

SUZANNE. We hold up our fingers to let them dry in the wind and say,

> Listen, listen, good Saint Phayre,
> Hear our wish and grant our prayer.

MARY. Is that all?

SUZANNE. Yes, that's all we *say*, but we have to stay here in complete silence for an hour afterwards. If we speak a single word the spell will be broken. Don't forget.

MARY. I won't. Get ready. The beam's nearly there. Oh, I wonder if it'll really come true. I can't believe it will.

SUZANNE. Of course it will. People have been here for centuries and wished. They wouldn't bother to come if there was nothing in it. Aunt Hester little knows what's in store for her.

MARY (*whispering*) Now, do you think?

SUZANNE (*whispering*) Yes. Now!

(*Both go to the well and dip their fingers, saying the rhyme solemnly*)

SUZANNE and MARY (*together*)
> With our fingers in your well,
> Good Saint Payre our wish we tell.

(*They look at each other very earnestly and repeat slowly*)

We wish that grown-ups and children change places.

(*They looked awed, take their fingers out and hold them in the air*)

> Listen, listen, good Saint Phayre,
> Hear our wish and grant our prayer.

THE WIZARD OF OZ

By Elizabeth Fuller Chapman
From the story by L. Frank Baum

Dorothy's home in Kansas has been destroyed by a cyclone and she finds herself with her dog, in the land of the Munchkins.

Scene—*Munchkin Farm.*

Dorothy (*sobbing*) Oh, Toto! That dreadful cyclone must have carried us from home. What *shall* we do?

(Toto *barks sadly, then runs over to the* Witch of the North *and* Munchkins *who are entering from* r. *He sniffs the Witch and runs back to Dorothy and whines*)

Witch (*bowing low to Dorothy*) You are welcome, most noble Sorceress, to the Land of the Munchkins. We are so grateful to you for having killed the wicked Witch of the East, and for setting our people free from bondage.

Dorothy (*in wonder and hesitation*) You are very kind, but there must be some mistake. I have not killed anything.

(Toto *barks, shaking head "no-no"*)

Witch (*laughingly*) Your house did anyway, and that is the same thing. See! There are her two shoes still sticking out under a block of wood.

Dorothy (*dismayed and frightened*) Oh, dear! Oh, dear! The house must have fallen on her. Whatever shall we do?

Toto (*cries*) Woof-woof.

Witch. There is nothing to be done. (*Calmly*)

Toto. Wuf-wuf—(*shaking head "no"*)

Dorothy. But who was she?

Witch. She was the wicked Witch of the East. She has held all the Munchkins in bondage for many years. Now they are all set free and are grateful to you for the favour.

Dorothy. Who are the Munchkins?

Witch. They are the people who lived in this land of the East where the Wicked Witch ruled.

Dorothy. Are you a Munchkin?

Witch. No; but I am their friend. When they saw the Witch of he East was dead they sent for me. I am the Witch of the North.

Dorothy. Oh gracious! Are you a real witch?

(Toto, *running in front of Dorothy, growls at the Witch*)

WITCH. Yes, indeed, but I am a good witch and the people love me.

DOROTHY (*frightened*) But I thought all witches were wicked.

WITCH. Oh, no! That is a great mistake. There are only four witches in all the Land of Oz and two of them, those who live in the North and South are good witches, while those of the East and West were indeed wicked; but now that you have killed one of them there is but one wicked witch in all the Land of Oz—the one who lives in the West.

DOROTHY. But Aunt Em told me that the witches were all dead years and years ago.

WITCH. Who is Aunt Em?

DOROTHY. She is my aunt who lives in Kansas where I come from.

WITCH (*thoughtfully*) I do not know where Kansas is. But tell me, is it a civilized country?

DOROTHY. Oh, yes.

TOTO. Wuf-wuf (*nodding head*)

WITCH. Then that accounts for it. In the civilized countries, I believe there are not any witches left, nor wizards, nor sorcerers, nor magicians. But you see, the Land of Oz has never been civilized, therefore, we still have witches and wizards amongst us.

DOROTHY. Who are the wizards?

WITCH (*whispering*) Oz himself is the Great Wizard. He is more powerful than all the rest of us together. He lives in the City of Emeralds.

(*The* MUNCHKINS *point to the shoes out of which the feet of the dead witch have disappeared entirely leaving only the shoes*)

See—the wicked Witch was so old that she dried up quickly in the sun. That was the end of her. But the silver shoes are yours and you shall have them to wear. (*Reaching down and picking up the shoes she shakes the dust out of them and hands them to* DOROTHY)

(TOTO *sneezes violently*)

The Witch of the East was proud of these silver shoes. There is some charm connected with them; but what that is, we never knew.

(DOROTHY *puts on the shoes*)

DOROTHY. I am anxious to get back to my aunt and uncle. Can you help me find my way?

THE WIZARD OF OZ

SCENE—*Munchkin Farm.*

DOROTHY *and* TOTO *walk to* R *and* TOTO *sniffing the Scarecrow barks suddenly.* DOROTHY *sees the* SCARECROW. *While she is looking earnestly at him, she is surprised to see him wink slowly at her. He nods.* TOTO *runs around him and barks.*

SCARECROW (*huskily*) Good day.
DOROTHY (*wonderingly*) Did you speak?
SCARECROW. Certainly. How do you do?
DOROTHY (*politely*) I'm pretty well, thank you. How do you do?
SCARECROW. I'm not feeling very well for it is very tedious being perched up here night and day to scare away crows.
DOROTHY. Can't you get down?
SCARECROW. No, for this pole is stuck up my back. If you will please take away the pole, I shall be greatly obliged to you.

(DOROTHY *lifts the* SCARECROW *off the pole. He falls down in a heap. She picks him up and places him on his feet again. He stretches and yawns*)

Thank you very much. I feel like a new man. (*He bows*) Who are you and where are you going?
DOROTHY. My name is Dorothy, and I am going to the Emerald City to ask the Great Oz to send me back to Kansas.
SCARECROW. Where is the Emerald City and who is Oz?
DOROTHY (*surprised*) Why, don't you know?
SCARECROW (*sadly*) No indeed, I don't know anything. You see I am stuffed, so I have no brains at all.
DOROTHY. Oh! I am awfully sorry for you.
SCARECROW. Do you think if I go to the Emerald City with you, that the Great Oz would give me some brains?
DOROTHY. I cannot tell, but you may come with me if you like. If Oz will not give you any brains, you will be no worse off than you are now.
SCARECROW. That is true. You see, I don't mind my legs and arms and body being stuffed because I cannot get hurt. If anyone treads on my toes or sticks pins into me, it doesn't matter, for I can't feel it. But I do not want people to call me a fool, and if my head stays stuffed with straw instead of with brains, as yours is, how am I ever to know anything?

(*He treads on* TOTO *who barks*)

DOROTHY. I understand how you feel. If you will come to me, I'll ask Oz to do all he can for you.

SCARECROW (*gratefully*) Thank you.

(TOTO *smells around the Scarecrow as if he suspects there might be a nest of rats in the straw, and he growls often in an unfriendly way*)

DOROTHY. Don't mind Toto, he never bites.

SCARECROW. Oh, I'm not afraid—he can't hurt the straw. Do let me carry that basket for you. I shall not mind it for I can't get tired. I'll tell you a secret. There is only one thing in the world that I am afraid of.

DOROTHY. What is that? The Munchkin farmer who made you?

SCARECROW (*whispering with finger on his lips*) No! It is a lighted match.

DOROTHY (*laughs and takes the Scarecrow by the hand*) Well, come on. Let's go!

They exit R, TOTO barking as CURTAIN falls.

CURTAIN

MADE AND PRINTED IN GREAT BRITAIN BY
LATIMER TREND AND CO. LTD, PLYMOUTH
MADE IN ENGLAND

ISBN 0 573 09032 7